AFTER DINNER SPEAKING

AFTER DINNER SPEAKING

Preparation
Weddings
Anniversaries
Business Speeches
40 pages of Quotes

Fawcett Boom

REED

First published 1991 by

Reed Books Pty Ltd
3/470 Sydney Road
Balgowlah NSW 2093

© 1991 The Watermark Press

National Library of Australia
Cataloguing-in-Publication Data

Boom, Fawcett
After Dinner Speaking

ISBN 0-7301-0368-4
9 780730 103684

Cover by Sophie Blackall
© Illustrations by Phil Somerville
Produced in Australia for the Publisher by
The Watermark Press, Sydney

Printed in Melbourne through The Book Printer

Contents

Age, Art, Music, Film, Theatre, Beauty,
Childhood & Parenthood, Drink, Economy,
Fashion, Feminism, Food, Cooks & Cooking,
History, Humanity, Knowledge, Law, Life,
Love, Marriage, Media, Politics, Religion,
Science, Technology, Sex, Travel, War

Introduction

We should really blame television. Takes and re-takes followed by hours of editing make everyone appear perfect. Speeches are witty, sharp and to the point because there is always a team of professional scriptwriters working away behind the scenes. Speakers are professionally dressed and professionally groomed.

Mistakes only happen in comedies or when the television reporter wants to make a politician appear a bumpkin.

Yet behind every professional appearance is a series of 'out takes' — these are the moments professionals would best forget. Moments when politicians say, "Aargh, what was the question again?" or film stars say "F*#@!" as a microphone falls in the soup sending a shower of hot liquid into a waiting lap.

'Live' speaking is a different matter altogether. Professionals who know the value of considerate camera operators, sensitive panel mixers, clever scriptwriters, complimentary make up artists and skilled editors turn into quivering wrecks at the thought of a live appearance. So where does that leave the amateur, the person who for the first time in their life is going to stand and make a speech in front of friends, family, co-workers or even enemies?

There's no point hiding from it — most people are terrified at the thought of speaking in public. Surveys have shown that most of us would rather fight lions bare handed than face a sea of after dinner revellers.

Don't be ashamed to admit (to yourself, at least) that the whole idea of public speaking is nerve-racking. To make this admission is the first step in the creation of a great — a memorable — after dinner speech.

Why? The nature of fear is an elusive thing to track down. A psychiatrist might even say that the fears experienced by people asked to speak in public are as varied as the people themselves. Not quite true.

There are only three things that cause fear of after dinner speaking. The first is the fear of saying or doing something that will make you look silly and the second is the fear of revealing something personal about yourself to strangers.

The third is that all people lack confidence in something they have not done before, don't know how to do, and have no way of practising without the possibility of making a mistake. This makes factors 1 and 2 all the more fearsome.

The last one can be handled quite simply by using this book to plan the occasion well and there are pretty good methods of practising and testing your progress before you too appear in public.

The first and second fears are more difficult to ignore because they are mainly irrational fears. Most of the first

— the fear of doing or saying something that will make you look silly — can be eliminated if the occasion is well organised (see Fear 3).

In fact, all your fears can be quickly eliminated if you:

1. learn what needs to be done

2. plan it well

3. rehearse it beforehand

4. prepare yourself for things that can go wrong and

5. stay sober until it's over

What makes this book different from any other book on Public Speaking? Again the answer is fear. Similar books will explain which words and phrases to use, the types of speech you may have to make or when it is tasteful to crack a joke and when it isn't.

There is only one reason a person, any person (yes, you too) would buy a book which has 'After Dinner Speaking' on the cover. It is because they've been asked to make a speech and suddenly the world has become a treacherous place filled with monsters and goblins. Hands become clammy and lips dry at the thought of standing in front of an audience and doing something as complicated as speaking. Terror strikes the heart of every person who has been asked to make an after dinner speech for the first time. Climb a mountain? Sure! Make a parachute jump? Certainly! Hand-feed cat biscuits to a Bengal Tiger? A cinch! But make a speech after dinner? Rambo never had it so tough!

Yet if you can speak to one person you can speak to 100, or 1000 or a million. There is no difference (well, to be truthful there is — but that's what this book is about). Most of us will speak to friends, family and strangers without a second thought. But only as long as we haven't been specially asked to speak to them. The instant we are asked to deliver a speech, family become enemies, friends strangers and strangers armed aliens waiting for a single excuse to gun you down. Mispronounce a single word, say something just a leeetle bit wrong and the earth will open up beneath you. Wrong. Instead, you'll still be there and you'll still have to face the music.

So this book will give you sufficient skills so that you can speak confidently after dinner. You may even enjoy speaking after dinner. In fact you could be on the brink of becoming a great after dinner speaker.

First it is necessary to understand the difference between speaking to someone and being asked to make a speech. Only then will you appreciate that there is very little difference between the two. Example. You're the innocent bystander when two cars collide. You watch the drama as drivers shout and tow trucks assemble and crowds of gawkers come and go. Finally a police officer asks for your account of the events well away from the drivers so you can say what needs to be said in privacy. This is a simple act of communication. You're speaking to another human and relating a narrative — a tale of woe in which there are good people and bad people and winners and losers. Then the summons arrives for you to attend court and do the same thing in front of a jury. Your knees turn to jelly. All because you are being asked to speak in public. Yet the story you must tell hasn't changed.

Another example. It is the end of a memorable meal at which your best friends announced their plans to marry. The time has been wonderful with fabulous conversations passing from one person to another as jokes against them both are told (some rude, crude and vulgar), memories jogged, nostalgia laid bare and everyone at the table enjoys and shares the love between them. Then a parent phones and asks you to give the major speech at the couple's wedding. Panic! Yet the occasion is likely to be little different from that memorable evening when the wedding was announced. In blind despair you rush to the nearest bookshop to seek a simple solution to the huge problem you imagine you're facing. Certainly there are some fine books on the subject of after dinner speaking. But they are few and far between. Mostly books on this subject continue to include forms of address for Royalty, Presidents and Archbishops (or Cardinals). Times have changed. The world is far less formal than it was when most after dinner speaking books were first written (before the 153rd rewrite in 1976). Also, people in power and great people have become so sheltered and protected from ordinary folk that you are unlikely to ever need the correct term for addressing the President of the USA or the Pope, unless you're a member of the secret police! Times *have* changed. The era when a thousand people would faint if you didn't know the difference between, "Your Grace" and "Your Excellency" has passed.

Today, politeness and respect have taken their rightful place in the speeches of those who must perform in public. Simple phrases, easy words and courteous expressions are now used instead of the fearsome ritual nonsense which was left over from Victorian times. In fact, public speaking has never been easier. This book has chapters on each of the things you will need to know to make a successful speech in public. From making sure that the public address system works to handling a heckler, from knowing when to start talking and when (and how) to finish. If you read this book carefully and act on what you have learnt, you will have little time for fear. You might even become an after dinner hero!

PREPARATION

Some of the sweetest sounds that a speaker can hear are the surprised ripple of laughter from the audience, the murmurs of approval at praise well deserved, and the firm hand of applause at the end of a speech, a sound of clapping that goes beyond the polite. The public speaker who has scored this appreciation can sit down happy. They have the reward not only of public acclaim, but also a sense of satisfaction for themselves, that they have done the job well.

To win these prizes you do not have to have the words of Shakespeare and the voice of Laurence Olivier. What is needed first is preparation, thorough preparation, and then just as importantly, picking the right guidelines for your speech according to your abilities and appropriate for the occasion.

Get Your Guidelines Right

'Guidelines' is the word to stick to. Some books on public speaking have more rules than the Tax Act. They warn sternly that unless all the rules are followed speakers will find themselves frozen on their feet, tongue-tied and lost. The truth is that people are different and occasions are different. You don't have to go into the forum loaded down with lead in your saddlebags, with a host of worries about what can go wrong. Just plan carefully, pick the right guidelines and you'll get it right.

The main point to accept before starting out is that public speaking is not just for the audience — it's for you. Getting a speech right is one of the great pleasures of life.

Traditions of Public Speaking

The sharing of memories and the sharing of understanding is the mark of the human community. History began with the stories of the first public speakers: the singers, the poets of the tribe. They too had to prepare and rehearse so that they could hold their audience. Long before there were books the speakers were the custodians of the developing culture. People came together whether at feasts during the long winter nights in Europe or under the starry desert skies. These occasions were social gatherings: feasts for marriages, the birth of children, the passing of the dead. The singers were expected to sing the praises of the tribe and its heroes, the families and their members. At times in history, such as the Victorian age, social occasions became overlaid with too much ritual and too many rules. Social functions were an excuse to exclude people rather than bring them together. Today we are much more relaxed about social functions and the appropriate dress for an occasion than we were a couple of generations ago. But it is true that when we come together for public events people still need speech to bind them together. On occasions of joy; like a marriage or a christening, or of sorrow; like a funeral, words are needed to celebrate or to heal.

Increasing Involvement

Public speaking has also found fresh territory. Once only the politicians or aspiring politicians dealt with social issues in meetings. Now many people are called upon to participate in gatherings that will help make important decisions on the future of their neighbourhood or their children's education. In business not only the senior executives but also the middle ranking executives are likely to find themselves playing a public speaking role. They may talk at the presentation of an award to a sporting club or school students, or to a business convention or in a public forum on controversial company policy. There is still the same necessity for thorough preparation and the selection of the right guidelines. A business speaker has to strive for authority in a way that a social speaker need not. The audience may look forward to the business speech with boredom (there is no such thing as a "free lunch") and the social speech with pleasure. Therefore flexibility is vital. Each new occasion presents a different challenge. Sometimes novice speakers find it hard to approach the barrier the first time around. Sometimes even veterans can feel edgy with a new audience. But speaking in public is a skill that most people can master. You don't need to go to the country's top drama school or spend time on a psychiatrist's couch. Preparation, planning and practice are the way to get it right.

Whether you do it once and get it right, or go on to do it a hundred times, you are going to find public speaking one of the joys of life.

17

Speaking At Social Events

Social public speaking covers a multitude of occasions. It can be a serious event like a marriage, christening, wedding anniversary, or funeral or on the lighter side, an engagement party or a buck's party, or a birthday celebration. Sometimes a speech by the nature of the occasion must be solemn, sometimes by another convention, flippant. There is a whole range of social functions which can be something in between, a combination of formality and some humour: an end-of-year prize-giving, the vote of thanks in a social club, the welcome to a visiting sporting team. There is one guideline which is common to all: preparation. There are two divisions of preparation: working out the context of the speech, who you are talking to, the physical layout of the venue, the conditions, the programme, and then all that being done the preparation of the speech itself.

Physical Preparation

It is no good preparing a speech on employment opportunities for school leavers for a group that is made up of senior citizens. Obvious enough, but how many times have you heard a speaker come along with a set speech out of line with the age group or composition of the audience? Too often. At an occasion like a wedding it is even more vital to find out about the make-up of the invited group before you speak. If half of them are zealous teetotallers they don't want jokes about the hangover this morning and the same forethought applies to all public speaking occasions.

Basic Questions For Any Speech

1. How many people may attend?
2. Where do they come from — e.g. at a wedding, what proportion from each side?
3. Who are they — e.g. age groups, occupations, etc.
4. Who is running the proceedings? What is his or her title — M.C., Chairperson, whatever. Talk to him or her directly or on the phone, tell them a little about yourself so they can introduce you. Ascertain whether they will control events or the events control them.

5. What is the size of the venue? Will the numbers fill it? If not in what proportion? This is very important. If a venue is packed then a mood will be easier to create and your speech will generally be more successful. If it is half-empty ask the organisers to move everyone to the front of the room to reduce the echoing emptiness of the half-filled venue.

6. List the names of all the people you must mention in your speech and write alongside each the names of a person or persons who can tell you something about them. It might be a simple detail or a short anecdote. You often draw blanks on this, but it's worth a try.

7. If someone you don't know is also speaking at the same event, phone to introduce yourself and sound them out on their speech. Do not be embarrassed at doing this. It is to your mutual benefit since no audience wants to hear two people getting up and saying exactly the same things.

8. Go to the venue and inspect it in person. Determine where you will speak from, standing at the table or at a podium. If you are speaking at a table is there a portable podium which you can use for your notes? Will there be sufficient lighting so you can read your speech?

9. Is there a microphone? If so, is it on a table or on a stand? How is it manipulated for height? Is there a clip-on microphone? If so politely insist on your preference for it, because venues often give people their older equipment, unless specifically asked. Try to test it out before the guests arrive to ensure that it does not give out one of those ear-piercing whines as soon as it is switched on.

10. If you can't get to the venue before the event discover what you can by phoning the Functions Manager or the person in charge of the venue.

Preparing and Delivering the Speech

The first thing to remember with most after dinner speaking is that you are addressing an audience that has something in common. At a wedding, they will know at least one of the couple. At a prize-giving they share an interest, e.g. children at the same school. At a sporting function they are bound together by a common loyalty to that sport.

The next advantage you have is that the audience is on your side, and that is a big plus. They really want to hear you so why not make the most of the opportunity and go home a hero! You've got your physical preparations right (page 00) now you can prepare your speech.

Basic Points For Any Speech

1. Work out how long it should be. In most cases brief is best. Fidel Castro would sometimes speak for half a day but we doubt that his audience were listening after the first ten minutes. Abraham Lincoln's address at Gettysburg probably lasted no longer than five minutes, and was delivered without the assistance of a microphone but it has gone down in history as one of the great speeches of all time. In contrast famous professional entertainers can seemingly hold an audience for

half an hour or more but they've got a team of backroom speech writers. You haven't. Now put your mind back to the weddings and other social events you have attended. The interested silence that pervaded the room as the speaker got up but then the increasing clatter of cutlery when they went on too long.

Should you put your watch on the podium or table? Nine times out of ten the answer is yes. You may well be surprised when you sit down at the end of your speech and realise you didn't even look at it. But the presence of a timekeeper provides a safety net. If by a mischance you have gone on too long and the M.C. intervenes, even if you think impolitely, don't resist. Wind up with a laugh.

2. Is the function one where you start with a list of names or would it be more appropriate for you bring the names in during the course of the speech? People love to hear themselves praised or thanked and if you can achieve this with style and wit your speech is a guaranteed success.

3. Even when you have started with a list of names you still need a carefully prepared opening. You must get the audience's attention. You've got to interest them. There are three broad choices:

(i) the summing up of the virtues of one or two people such as the bride and groom, or of an institution e.g. short history of the school, college, hospital.

(ii) a suitable quote for the occasion which can be light-hearted or not;

(iii) a joke which must be carefully selected and tried out on a trusted friend.

Whatever the introduction, it should be just that. The start is not the time for a shaggy dog story.

4. The body of the speech. This should expand on the virtues of everyone involved. At a wedding not only are the bride and groom praised, but also their families and their friends. Then praise can be given to the quality of the food (if prepared by a friend or family member who is present), the floral decorations and so on. In sport the shared achievement of the players and their supporters can be stressed. In contemporary society most people will not have had the sort of background, such as geographic isolation or institutional membership, that binds small communities together. So the social occasion provides an important experience of community. What goes with this is praise, not flattery, but deserved praise, and call it just that. The audience will feel happy to hear of the generosity of parents and the solidarity of friends. When you research your speech you are looking for good things to say about the people you are going to mention.

5. The conclusion, the wind up. Sometimes this is easy — a toast. Sometimes a good quote is just right. If you are using your own words, try them out on a friend. The closing words are particularly important. They should not be a garbled or hurried sentence. You can say something about the people you have mentioned earlier, there is no harm in repeating in different words some of the praise you have already given.

6. To write or not to write out the speech. There is no golden rule on this, you have to do what makes you comfortable. If you are a novice speaker you may think you can press on without notes, impromptu. Maybe you've been in a profession like a teacher or racing commentator where you talk a lot and you think that you can do it in another forum. Good luck. It may be that the speech, by consent, is to be very short. There are other participants at a wedding, who may have made it very clear that they don't want anything said except the toast. Then holding a piece of paper is a bit pointless. Conversely if you feel that you can only give a speech with a text, then have a text. Just ignore those people who say you should never have a full text on a social occasion, but try the speech out on a friend and ask them to criticise you if it sounds too stilted.

There is one social occasion when for almost any speaker, novice or veteran, a written text is the most sensible course, and that is at a funeral where you are being asked to give a tribute to the deceased. Writing out a funeral speech is sensible. If you are being asked to perform that role you may well feel a surge of grief as you speak their name, and that is very human. Having a written speech in front of you will help you to go on. Your listeners will feel the same so you need to avoid any gaps in the speech which may upset them.

For that occasion or any other if you are going to read a full text, get it typed, double-spaced. If possible have it typed in big type (most photocopiers these days will blow up a text). Using large type has got nothing to do with eyesight. Presidents, prime ministers and leaders of industry, all read from texts with big type because they know it helps, especially with indoor lighting.

A final comment on writing out a speech. All those speeches which have been recorded for posterity were obviously written out. They were probably carefully rehearsed too!

7. To pin the notes or the sheets together or to leave them loose (don't use clips, they slip). This may seem a trivial point but in fact it is quite important. Your decision depends on whether you've got a podium and if so how wide it is or whether you are standing, holding your speech or notes in your hand.

   If the podium is wide enough then picking up the finished sheet, turning the page over and placing it to one side makes sense. If it's narrow then the pin and folding over the sheets is the way to go. Picking up the page and putting it underneath the pile is okay if you've only got two pages. When there's more something can go wrong. This may seem a minor point, but many promising orations have been ruined by the speaker fumbling after pages which have gone astray. If you have any hesitation then pin or staple the pages of your speech together.

8. If you're not going to take the full text then you can still use paper or big cards. It's wise to have your introductory comments and your closing comments in full. As well you should have your name list, preferably with a memory trigger word or phrase, e.g. Alice Jones (bride's

mother) — hospitality famous.

9. When you arrive, seek out the MC or chairperson to re-establish contact. Particularly at a function like a wedding, confirm the time when you will be speaking. Again assess how far he or she will be in control. The M.C. at a social function where people are eating and drinking is important not only for the function's success but also for your success.

Later when the time comes for you to speak you will have to decide whether to nudge the MC about introducing you. Sometimes even in the best ordered world, functions can get rowdy, and then it might be prudent to suggest going on early. Whatever you decide, timing will always be vital.

10. Put your napkin on the table well before you're due to stand up. Again a little thing but you can be thrown by getting to your feet in a hurry.

11. Set up a glass of water if you can. This is easier to do at your table but more difficult when standing at a podium. It's a useful prop to pick up if you get stuck. Don't use your beer or wine glass, because some wit is sure to take the opportunity to say something funny. The advantage of water is that it is not at all funny.

12. You are on your feet, but wait for the MC to hush people, then move to the standing podium. A warning for novices: no eye contact with anyone in the audience. If you are tempted to look for a particular friend to catch their eye so that they can give you courage, don't. Actors have a phrase for this danger. In a small theatre

to catch someone's eye is to risk being "thrown out of character". You are talking to the whole gathering, not just your friend, and that means you don't wink at him or her when you have a funny line either. The rest of the audience may feel excluded. Don't stare fixedly into mid-air; a simple trick is to look at each of the distant corners of the room alternately.

13. Another problem for a novice: don't listen to yourself. It's an odd thing about standing up, even without a microphone, you will find your voice coming back to you. First time speakers are often thrown by this. Be warned, anticipate it and ignore it.

14. You stutter, even though the last time you stuttered was in first grade. Keep going and don't joke about it. No one will have noticed.

15. At the end when you are proposing the toast, turn to face the subject of the toast. Don't wait around for applause, walk straight back to your table or sit down.

16. Smile when you are seated. Don't ask the person next to you; how you went. They may have been asleep before you started or have left their hearing aid off. Don't be downcast if people don't rush up to you afterwards and congratulate you on your speech. Most people don't congratulate others unless — you're right — they themselves are giving a speech.

SOCIAL

PUBLIC

SPEAKING

Weddings

Weddings are generally happy social occasions when the whole family comes together to celebrate the union of two people and to wish them luck for their future together. Some are small, intimate affairs with just the immediate family and a few close friends while others are lavish parties involving the gathering of the entire clan.

Whatever the size of the guest list, speeches play an important role at weddings. They may be delivered at the ceremony or reception. Speeches at weddings vary according to the tone of the event i.e. whether it is formal or informal. They also take into consideration the accepted customs of different religions and cultures.

One thing a speechmaker at a wedding can always count on is that the guests are on your side. They want your speech to be a success. It is a joyful event so ideally your speech should unify the crowd so that everyone feels part of the occasion. One of the best ways to unite people from different age groups, interests and economic circumstances is to make them all feel part of the event by delivering a lighthearted speech peppered with funny anecdotes, jokes or one-liners. Humour creates a friendly and relaxed atmosphere and is the essential ingredient in any wedding speech, formal or informal.

A word of caution, however. Use humour in moderation. Nothing becomes more tiresome or rings as false as a constant stream of one-liners or bad jokes. Also, avoid jokes that may cause embarrassment or hurt to anyone present. Remember you are there to flatter the bride and groom not to boost your own ego by displaying a spiteful wit. Bear in mind too the ages of the guests. A prim eighty year old grandmother will not appreciate a smutty joke about the bride and neither will many others. In fact, sexual innuendoes should be avoided at all costs — they are usually tasteless and fall completely flat.

Well-known quotes from famous people may draw a laugh or at the very least add interest to a speech. And if you have time to do a bit of research at the library you could find out what other famous historical events took place on the same day. Film stars and people in the entertainment industry are great sources for quotes about marriage — most have attended more than one of their own weddings so they usually have plenty of thoughts on matrimony. Turn to the back of the book for some quotable quotes on marriage and love to give you some ideas.

If you do not have time for research or lack the skills of witty comedians don't waste too much time agonising over funny one-liners. It is probably best to leave humour well alone and concentrate on being sincere. Remember the original reasons behind wedding speeches — to give thanks, good-wishes to the newlyweds and praise where due. Thus you should include thanks to the hosts and other organisers as well as honouring the bride and groom and acknowledging the presence of any special guests.

Following the rules of etiquette at a formal wedding will make sure that nobody is left out or offended. However, these rules were devised when weddings were a once in a lifetime event. Times have changes since then. Some women choose careers above marriage although others still consider marriage a career in itself. Many men and women marry more than once. Some never marry. Etiquette has not quite caught up with these social changes but most of the following rules are flexible, like everything else about modern weddings. Rules can be altered to accommodate a wedding where, for instance, the bride is given away by her mother or where the bride makes a speech on behalf of herself and her husband. It happens!

Basic Etiquette in Wedding Speeches

Many people consider large weddings to be an organisational nightmare. Certainly, they require a lot of careful thought and planning. The success of the day relies on plenty of hard work behind the scenes.

The same applies to speeches. Never leave the preparation of a speech to the last minute. Find out when you are to make it, how long it should be and plan, plan, plan.

The traditional order of speeches at formal weddings is quite logical. The first speech is generally made by a close friend of the newlyweds, who ends his or her speech by calling for a toast to the bride and groom. The groom must then reply on behalf of himself and his bride. During his speech he should thank both his in-laws, who traditionally will have provided the venue and paid for the reception.

He should end his speech with a toast to the bridesmaids and/or Matron of Honour. Sometimes the bride may speak as well as her husband or instead of him. The best man replies on behalf of the bridesmaids and he too may end with a toast to the hosts. Finally, the best man reads out the messages, faxes and telegrams from absent friends or relatives.

The first two speeches are the most important.

The first speaker should begin by thanking the M.C. and welcoming the guests. This should be followed by some complimentary remarks about the newlyweds and their families before launching into a short anecdote about the couple. Any quotes or sayings about marriage should follow here. The speechmaker should then expand on some stories about the family he knows best, taking care to include some flattering remarks about the other side of the family as well. If the speaker is unacquainted with the background of one of the couple it would pay to ask a few questions beforehand. Finally, the first speech winds up with the speaker wishing the couple happiness for the future and proposing a toast to the bride and groom.

The response by the groom or bride to the first speaker is his or her chance to express his or her gratitude for the smooth running of the day. They should begin by thanking the M.C. and the first speaker and then both sets of parents. Next thanks go to the best man, the guests and the people who arranged the flowers and the cake. Finally, thanks are given to the bridesmaids for their help and a toast is proposed to them.

To oversee the smooth running of these proceedings there is generally an M.C. who will ensure everyone comes in on cue. At most formal weddings a trusted friend, preferably with a loud voice, is appointed to this position. Their role is to make sure the event proceeds without a hitch and their duties include announcing guests on the receiving line to the wedding party, announcing dinner and introducing speakers. They must also make sure that each speaker knows the order in which they are appearing to save last minute confusion. Often the M.C. will also have the back-up support of a senior family member.

Most speeches take place after the meal has finished as it is easier to hold guests' attention while they are still letting their food settle. It is up to the bride and groom to decide whether they want the speeches to come before or after the cutting of the cake and serving of coffee.

The timing of speeches should be given careful consideration. If they are held too early it is possible that latecomers will miss most of them or disrupt them as they arrive. Speeches too late into the night suffer because the audience is usually restless by this stage and are probably a little rowdy after wining and dining.

Research

Like other forms of public speaking, you can never do too much research when preparing a wedding speech. Research is the key to success. Before you begin, it is a good idea to ask yourself first why you have been asked to make the speech. This may give you an indication of what is expected in the tone of your speech. If you are an older person, your speech should perhaps give gentle advice while if you are known for being funny, your speech should have a humorous approach.

Next, decide on the length of your speech. Remember quality is better than quantity. Instead of making an incredibly long-winded speech, keep it short, sweet and sincere. Some speechmakers make the mistake of inflicting every incident from the bride's past, as well as the couple's progress to the altar, upon the captive audience at a wedding reception. Do not fall into this trap. Several well chosen anecdotes are all that are necessary for a quick trip down memory lane. Be brief. Five minutes is a good length for most speeches. Any shorter and it may seem rude; too long and the guests will be bored. Bear in mind that formal weddings generally require longer speeches while informal events are open to interpretation.

There are four basic things to remember when thinking about a wedding speech. Of course, these pointers should be read alongside the chapter on preparation.

1. Begin your research by setting yourself a theme which you can expand in the main part of your speech.

2. Collect anecdotes about the bride and groom by talking to their parents, relatives and close friends. After all, it is safe to assume that everyone will be interested in the bride and groom and their families. Sprinkle these throughout your speech so as to keep the audience's interest.

3. Remember to strike a balance between personal and

general material. Too many 'I remember when..' and many guests will feel excluded. By using the more general phrase 'I am told that...' you should make all the guests feel at ease.

4. Do not overdo it. Some people spend too much time researching and realise too late that they have not left themselves long enough to actually write and edit the speech. You do not need pages and pages of notes. A handful of pleasant anecdotes is all that is necessary to keep the audience listening to your every word.

Writing

A wedding speech should reflect both the personality of the speaker and the tone of the occasion at the same time. A short, low-key speech is not really suitable for a formal wedding. On the other hand, if you are not an experienced public speaker it is best to keep your speech on a fairly casual and friendly level, even at a formal occasion. There is nothing worse than hearing someone stumbling over awkward words and phrases. Much better to be yourself and make an honest, heartfelt speech that you feel comfortable with.

There are a few golden rules to remember when writing your speech. For people who have already developed their own method of writing these pointers should be kept in the back of their minds. Those with little writing experience, however, will find them useful guidelines.

1. Work through your notes and select the bits you would like to use.

2. Arrange them in order, chronologically or otherwise.

3. Make a list of the thanks and the toast and any other important point that must be included in your speech.

4. Begin writing your opening remarks. Once you have established your lead, the rest of the speech should flow on. Do not be discouraged if it takes you several hours to settle on an opening that you are happy with. Once you have decided on this the rest should fall into place.

5. Avoid writing anything negative or critical. The last thing you want to do is make the groom or bride look foolish on their big day. Much better to abide by the old adage: if in doubt, leave it out.

6. Do not put in any rude jokes or sexual innuendoes. They generally go down like a lead balloon.

7. Most importantly, write the speech as though you were having a conversation with a small group of people. Delete any sentences which are too long and leave you gasping for breath at the end. Your speech will be most successful if it sounds spontaneous. Read it aloud several times to ensure that if flows easily.

Delivery

It is obvious that the better prepared you are, the more relaxed you will be when you finally deliver your speech. If you have followed the research and writing steps listed above you should have no problems. However, if you feel butterflies stirring in your stomach when the M.C. calls your name, do not panic. Take a couple of long, deep breaths and make sure you are standing comfortably before you begin. The following points should only act as guides for your big moment.

1. Before you begin reading your speech, check that everyone can hear you. On family occasions such as weddings there are usually elderly people present who may not always have good hearing. Ask people at the back of the room to shout out 'yes' if they can hear you or 'speak up' if they cannot.

2. When reading your speech, speak loudly and clearly throughout. Do not hurry your speech or fade away at the end of the sentence as you hastily look down at your notes for the next line. Look up and do not mumble.

3. Pause after telling a joke. If you rush on to the next part of your speech it will not be heard. Allow time for the laughter to subside before you continue.

4. If the venue has a microphone, adjust it to your height before you begin your speech. Many a promising oration has been ruined by the speaker fiddling with the microphone in the middle of their speech because the audience's attention goes to the equipment instead of the words being spoken. Remember too that microphones are very sensitive instruments. Even moving the chord around will often produce a distracting amount of what is called mike noise.

5. Do not put your mouth so close to the microphone that your 'p's' pop and words blare out in a distorted fashion. Instead, stand about half an arm's length away and speak just over the top of the microphone head.

Turn away if you have to sneeze, clear your throat or cough as the microphone will magnify all of these sounds.

6. Never race through your speech as though you cannot wait to sit down again. Make a conscious effort to go slow. Take a breath between sentences and where there are natural pauses. Remember that it only seems slow to you and that a slower speech adds emphasis.

7. If you discover when practising aloud that your voice sounds monotonous try varying it by giving emphasis to certain words. You may even mark key words in your speech. All this may sound phoney to you but it will keep the guests interested in what you are saying and believe me, it sounds a lot better than a dull drone.

Engagement Parties

In some countries an engagement or betrothal is a bigger celebration than the actual wedding, especially in Europe. Sometimes a huge party is thrown to mark the announcement that a young couple are now attached. This tradition is quite logical as a big engagement celebration allows the two families and friends to be introduced to each other.

In other parts of the world, the emphasis on the engagement rather than the wedding may be because the young couple are still studying or saving for their new life together. A big party gives the future bride a chance to show off her engagement ring and the young couple may receive presents to help them set up their new home.

Engagements are usually the responsibility of the bridegroom's parents while the bride's parents take care of the wedding. It would hardly be fair if the bride's father had to foot the bill for both an engagement party and a wedding, especially if they took place in the same year. It would be like paying for two weddings.

Although an engagement party may turn out to be a grander affair than the actual wedding, speeches are generally shorter and less formal than at a wedding reception. Indeed, there is a lesser air of formality at an engagement as the main job of the speakers is to introduce the young couple to the guests, express pleasure at the engagement and wish them all happiness. One of the parents of the future bride or groom, or whoever is host of the occasion, may then take the floor to offer a few words on the auspicious occasion.

Buck, Stag and Hen Parties

Many cultures have some device, some party or gathering, even athletic contests, where those about to be married let off steam and say goodbye to the single life. By tradition these are far from solemn affairs but an attempt at good taste is still appropriate. A good guideline is for nothing to be done or said that one partner could not tell the other later.

These parties are traditionally held the night before the wedding. However, this infamous evening of revelry has occasionally jeopardised a wedding. There are many stories of the groom and his best man being arrested for disorderly behaviour at the end of a wild evening or being stranded almost naked at some remote spot; or even placed on an overnight express train to another city. The idea of course is to prolong his bachelorhood but such events inevitably cause worry and distress to many other people. Sometimes the groom has arrived late to the church or, in the worst possible scenario, not even shown up. For this reason many brides or family members now insist that the buck's night is held at least a couple of days before the wedding to prevent anything spoiling the big day.

As far as speeches go, informality now mostly prevails. A popular device for organisers of a buck's party is to go around the room asking friends to tell stories about the groom from school, through to any tertiary education, work situations, sporting clubs etc. To suit the lively atmosphere of the night, humour should be the main ingredient of these speeches. But strike a balance between good taste and poking fun at the groom. Do not tell jokes that are embarrassing to the groom or that may get back to the bride and hurt her, possibly damaging their relationship.

Your speech on this night will also be a good indication to the bride or groom that you can be relied upon to fulfil your duties well as best man or bridesmaid at their wedding. While there is no need to labour over your speech for weeks in advance, an ad lib speech will not do either—unless you are an incredible raconteur. Select a story about the bridegroom carefully and give a little thought to how you are going to tell it.

Shower teas operate in much the same way. The name shower implies being 'showered with gifts' but they are still important social events. The host or hostess goes around the room asking each guest to recount a tale about the bride-to-be. These little speeches should be brief and witty. Often today guests come from different places and times in the future bride's life, so such anecdotes help everyone present to get to know each other and create a sense of warmer community.

It is up to the bride to decide whether she wants to hold a shower tea or have a hens' night, which is usually the wilder of the two. Some may choose to have both — in this case the shower tea is usually held a couple of weeks before the hens' night. Shower teas are designed to acquire gifts which will help set up the couple's new home, especially the kitchen. But whatever the future bride chooses, lively and amusing speeches will be the order of the day. Do not say anything that will hurt her feelings. Her last night or afternoon as a single woman surrounded by friends should be a happy event.

Christenings

Christenings are significant religious ceremonies involving the baptising, welcoming of the child into the church and naming of the child. They are generally small and informal affairs with just the immediate family, relatives and a few close friends in attendance.

As far as speeches go, the toast to the small child was once invariably made by the godfather, but it is now accepted that it may equally be made by the godmother. Godparents are selected with the utmost care by the child's parents. They are expected to guide the child spiritually and usually give a christening present of enduring value such as silver. They must also remember to send presents every birthday and Christmas.

The toast was once invariably made by the godfather, but it is now accepted that it may equally be made by the godmother. As a christening party is generally informal it is best to keep speeches as brief as possible.

Talk a little about the baby, its name and why it was chosen, as well as its brothers and sisters, part of the larger family. Name them all, because siblings can be a little put out by a newcomer. Don't tell them you are sure that they will love their baby brother/sister — too many people have probably said that today — but give them the attention of being known by name so that they feel important and part of the occasion.

Mention the grandparents and note if this is the first grandchild or if not give the score. It is still prudent to check with the parents first on this because some grandparents, usually the more youthful, don't like their new role being talked about.

If the celebrant is there, mention him or her too.

Wedding Anniversaries

This sort of celebration is not as common today as they were once, even with longer lives, but an anniversary celebration should be just that — a celebration.

If a couple have lived together this long and want to have a special function then it is a sentimental, romantic occasion and a good public speaker should take his tone from the occasion. You can certainly speak longer than at a christening, or even a wedding.

The most important thing to remember about your speech is to plan. At no time is research more important than now. The more reminiscing the better. After all, if everyone is there to celebrate the couple's long marriage it is guaranteed that they will want to hear about their life together. Many of the younger relatives too will be pleased to find out more about older members of the extended family.

Talk to the couple's old friends. Find out how they met and finally got together. Some of the most touching speeches are those where the speaker recounts what the couple's first impressions were of each other. Was she swept off her feet by his charms or did she find him too arrogant when they first met? Did he win her over with persistence or was he indifferent to her at first? Were they ever separated for long periods of time? Did they send love letters to each other? Was their relationship more an affair of the mind, did they argue a lot and do they still?

Some points to bear in mind include:-

1. Where were they married? Here or in another town/city? Is the church, synagogue or temple still there? Is there anyone present who was at the wedding?

2. Where did they go to school/college/university and what careers did they follow. Any notable academic, business or sporting achievements. Are any of their contemporaries present?

3. The family, the children, grandchildren and great-grandchildren. Have all their names on a card. This may be one of the few occasions when all the generations of an extended family get together. After the family read the best wishes from those who are not unable to attend.

4. The couple themselves. The home they made for the children, their loyalty to their friends. The toast.

Twenty-First Birthdays

These are not as widespread as they were once. The key to the door is now given, if not taken, much earlier. But many families still like the traditional twenty-first as a sign of the true adulthood of their son or daughter. Formal dress is usually worn on this occasion although these days it is common practice to set a fancy dress theme for the party.

The general atmosphere is lighthearted and speeches should reflect this. If there is a sit-down dinner or buffet speeches should be made after the desert course has finished. The first speech is usually made by the father or mother of the twenty-one year old. He or she should recount one or two of their favourite anecdotes about their daughter or son's growing up and end by expressing delight at their coming of age.

The main speech should be given by a close friend of the birthday person who has a range of anecdotes to show him or her in a good light. This is usually preferable to the parental speech which often embarrasses the son or daughter with references to their childhood behaviour. Friends' speeches may include funny stories about their time at school, the birthday person's sporting achievements or holidays they have been on together. Jokes are an essential part of a twenty-first speech. If the speaker has a talent for rhyme or is a natural comedian the speech can take the form of a funny poem. Some speakers with musical talents may even deliver their speech as a song while strumming their guitar or playing the piano. There is a lot of room for improvisation but remember the golden rule for speaking at public occasions. Be brief. To wind up the speaker should refer quickly to the parents, thanking them fulsomely on behalf of the guests.

The birthday person responds and should speak at rather more length about his or her parents, expressing personal gratitude. He or she should also have prepared a list of friends and relatives who have helped. These days the twenty-first is more for the older people than the younger people, so the birthday person should not go through a long catalogue of their friends, but limit themselves to one or two, so as not to overshadow the older generation.

Bar Mitzvah

The Bar Mitzvah celebrates the coming of age for Jewish boys and girls. At twelve girls are regarded as adults while for boys turning thirteen marks their passage to maturity. They become Barmitzvah, 'son of duty'. To celebrate, a Bar Mitzvah ceremony is held for boys while the relatively modern Bat Mitzvah is staged for girls. Both will have prepared for the occasion by completing special studies in the history and religion of Jewish people. On the day they read from the *Torah,* a section of the Hebrew bible meaning divine teaching. This reading is held in the synagogue and from then on they are expected to obey all Jewish laws. Afterwards often elaborate parties are held in their honour and attended by relatives and friends.

Boys and girls usually attend two schools when growing up, their ordinary daytime school and a Hebrew school in the evenings and on Sunday mornings. There they learn to speak Hebrew well enough to read from prayers during synagogue services. This is also in preparation for the Bar Mitzvah as they must read in Hebrew from the *Torah*. On the big day, a boy kisses the fringe of his prayer shawl before he chants or reads from the *Torah* and only ever touches it with this fringe as the scrolls are never handled by hand in case they become dirty or damaged. He may then be publicly addressed and congratulated by the Rabbi on behalf of the congregation. Sometimes he may lead the congregation in prayer. Girls participate in a similar ceremony at their Bat Mitzvah but at old fashioned synagogues are not allowed to read from the *Torah*.

Public speaking at a Bar Mitzvah is very ritualised and formula speeches are the appropriate address at the synagogue. Speeches at the party afterwards are a matter of choice and are more open to personal interpretation. The father of the boy or girl may make a short speech thanking everyone for sharing in the occasion, congratulating their child on coming of age and wishing them well in their adult life and in the continuation of their Jewish studies. The Barmitzvah or Batmitzvah should respond briefly by acknowledging the first speech and thanking those close to him or her as well as those responsible for his or her religious education.

Funerals

No matter what culture or religion, funerals and burials have always been important ceremonial rituals. Even primitive humans observed some form of ceremony at burials. Some people offered gifts to the dead as it was believed that the dead were going on a long journey from which they would never return. Hence the wonderful treasures found in the tombs of the Egyptian Pharaohs. Indeed, some of the wonders of the world, like the Great Pyramids of Egypt and the Taj Mahal in India, are magnificent memorials to the dead.

Today, however, simplicity is the general rule that governs most funerals. Wreaths of flowers are the most pleasing and accepted way of showing respect for the dead and sympathy for the family although on occasions there may be a request that no flowers be sent. It is wise to find this out from the funeral director beforehand. Speeches should reflect the sombre mood of the occasion. Be as brief and sincere as possible and remember to extend sympathy to the family of the deceased.

To be asked to give a eulogy is a great act of trust from the bereaved family, either to one of its own members or a friend. It may be delivered at the graveside, in a church, a crematorium chapel, or sometimes at home. In many instances the priest has already given an address at either of these places and if he knew the deceased may well have spoken personally about him or her. Therefore the person giving the eulogy should check with the clergyman beforehand to avoid overlap.

The speaker should also contact the funeral director to make it clear to the funeral director that the family have asked you to speak, because in a stressful situation people sometimes forget to pass on their decisions. Speaking aids such as a microphone are not always available, so the eulogist has to be ready to speak more loudly, although at the same time a conversational tone is to be recommended. As noted elsewhere, it is almost always desirable to speak from a prepared text. A suitable quotation is a good opening, perhaps from a piece of verse, or a hymn, which the deceased is known to have liked. There is a whole section of general quotes at the end of this book. After the opening a straightforward chronological account of the deceased's life should suffice: mention their birth, education, marriage, family, war service, work, recreational activities, organisations belonged to, etc. Then something flattering about the person themselves is appropriate, their life with their family. One telling anecdote is all that is needed, not a string of stories. You should also mention something about their values, such as the deceased was a respected family man or a wonderful mother.

If their death was the result of a protracted illness it is appropriate to acknowledge this by saying something like "the deceased's health had declined in the past couple of years" and to make some comment about how they coped bravely. However this should be checked with members of the family who sometimes cannot bear any reference to illness. The conclusion should be a tribute to the surviving partner and/or other members of the family in their time of sorrow.

It is <u>not</u> the place of the eulogist to go beyond the appointed task and speak of religious matters. His or her job is to pay tribute to the dead and help the mourners for a little time to deal with their loss. The eulogists should not put themselves in the foreground. If the speaker is not a member of the family and the speech is given at home a member or representative of the family will reply briefly to thank him or her and all the others who have attended.

After the funeral it is appropriate to give or send the text of the eulogy to the family.

AWARDS

Award Presentation and Acceptance

Awards have been in existence for a long time. The custom of giving awards for sporting excellence, for example, has been followed since the Olympic Games began in 776 B.C. But even before that the playwrights of ancient Greece were honoured before a crowd with awards.

Everyone has, at one time or another in their lives, attended an award-giving ceremony, even if it was only the end of year speech night at school. However, there are many other award nights in such areas as sport as well as cultural and civic matters.

More and more common these days are the award dinners which people attend because they do not want to cause offence. These functions are usually little more than a public relations exercise where the award recipient extols the virtues of the company which he or she represents.

Whatever the occasion may be, the general guidelines for preparing and giving a good speech apply to any occasion, although award-giving functions have tended to create their own protocol. Sometimes this can work against you if you do not inject a little of your own personality into the speech. Remember the audience has heard it all before: the singing of the recipient's praises and the 'few words' as the award or prize is handed over. Try and add some colour by using fresh phrases instead of well-worn clichés. However, do not fall into the trap of being flowery and overly sentimental. Gushing praise always rings false. Sincerity and a nicely-termed compliment should suffice.

Presentation Speech

If you stick by the formula (see below) for making presentation speeches you should have no problems on the big day or night.

The whole point of making a presentation speech is to honour the recipient and praise him or her for their accomplishments before handing over the award. Your speech will be successful if you manage to remember everyone involved in the few minutes you have.

Of course the most important person is the recipient. However, take time out to learn something about the background of the person so that you are honouring them and feeding the audience's curiosity at the same time. You should keep the following four points in the back of your mind when you write your speech:

1. Mention why the presentation is being made.

2. Give a few personal details about the recipient and praise him or her for their achievement.

3. Explain how honoured you feel to have been asked to present the award.

4. Describe what the award is. It may be a statue or a plaque, a holiday or any other number of things.

Acceptance Speech

Perhaps the most well-known examples of acceptance speeches are those heard at the Academy Awards in the United States every year. This Hollywood extravaganza is broadcast live and is avidly watched by millions of star-spotters around the world every year.

Yet producing the Oscars, as the Awards are otherwise known, is far from glamorous. In the past the show has often run overtime, thus exceeding the budget, because acceptance speeches were too long. The producers realised that not only did acceptances take up valuable time but it

was boring for the viewers and audience alike to listen to someone slowly reading down their seemingly interminable list of thanks. Nowadays everyone nominated for an award is given a strict length for their speech. If they go on too long they face being humiliated by the start of the background music which gradually drowns them out if they continue to try and be heard above it.

Make your acceptance speech short, sweet and to the point. If you remember this golden rule of speechmaking you should impress everyone and offend no-one by leaving them out accidentally. Bear in mind that simple thanks is all that is required. If you observe the following points you should have no problems.

1. Express your appreciation of the award and acknowledge the honour.
2. Thank the presenter.
3. Give a quick thanks to family, friends, your company or profession if they have given you assistance.
4. Finish up by expressing what the award means to you and say something about how it will spur you on to even greater heights.

High School and University Graduations

High school graduation parties are very common in the United States and given the spread of American cultural influences they are now occurring more frequently in other countries too. The same procedures apply for a high school graduation as for a university graduation party.

The parents share the spotlight with the graduate. The function exists to acknowledge the parental sacrifices as much as to applaud the graduate's achievements.

The father usually gives a brief speech of congratulation to the child. He should acknowledge any past teachers who are present and any relatives or friends who have had special influence. The graduate should respond by thanking the parents for their material and emotional support, as well as acknowledging other siblings.

It is customary for a close friend of the graduate to give the closing speech. They can talk in a lighthearted or even flippant way about the successful person of the day but they should be sure to conclude by reinforcing the message of gratitude to the parents.

School Prize-Giving

In the past, most guest speakers at school speech days were not novice speakers. Often they played a role in public life e.g. politician or mayor, which demanded regular speech-making. But there is an increasing tendency to bring in speakers from the community, perhaps a social worker from the local youth refuge or a leading light in the sporting community.

Sometimes the guest speaker hands out the prizes as well. The guest should do some research to link the school with his or her subject.

The youth refuge social worker should find out if any past students have become social workers; the sporting leader should refer to any former student who has gained distinction in his or her sport or any other.

Apart from the public figure or community speaker there is another feature category of school speech day address, that from a former student. In that case it is wise not to talk just about teachers; students are just as likely to be interested in how the school has changed physically. Some speakers choose to take a nostalgic path whereas others prefer to talk about education. The quotes at the end of this book are relevant for that kind of speech.

Sporting awards

In individual events, such as swimming and athletics, awards are usually given on the day. However, athletes may be called upon to speak at an end of year dinner or function. In team sports such as football or cricket, dinners or drinks parties that bring together players, administrators, supporters and sponsors, are now common. The usual form is an address from the chairperson with a toast to the club seconded by the captain or a spokesperson for the players. Both the chairperson and the players spokesperson will acknowledge the vital role of supporters. Some clubs adopt the practice of a separate toast for the supporters and/or sponsors.

The chairperson can usually use his or her speech to say something about the history of the club. Such speeches are usually expected to be brief. Where awards are given to individual players, e.g. best and fairest, it is customary for the recipient to say a few words.

Civic Awards

These are usually presided over by an experienced public speaker such as the mayor. The recipient makes a short speech and as such awards are very often given for community leadership, others will have been involved, so the speech provides the award winner with an occasion to acknowledge their help. The local historical society and in many municipalities the local libraries' historical sources can provide material to round out such a speech.

Cultural Awards

There are a myriad of cultural awards now and they are usually handed out by experienced public speakers. However guest speakers from the arts are often asked to give an address and the recipients are also expected to make a grateful acknowledgment. Where it is an institution involved, e.g. a local theatre group, it is appropriate to name those involved in the work of the group and to acknowledge the help of any local business sponsors. As with civic awards the speaker should contact the local historical society or library which can often provide something extra for the speech, an historical perspective which gives the opportunity to pay tribute to the founders of the group. Other sources for historical references are the early minute books, if they are available.

At another level, state and national cultural awards, the keynote addresses are usually given by experienced public speakers. It is customary for the recipients to say a few brief words thanking the donor and their family and perhaps a few others. It is not a good idea to have a long string of names. Cultural audiences can be quite as restive as football club gatherings.

Visiting Delegations, Teams, etc.

For many people their introduction to public speaking will take place at the reception for a visiting delegation or team, which may be a service club, sister city, sporting or cultural group. The group may come from overseas, another state or city or town.

The speaker should check out the venue as for other social functions, see pages 13-22. When researching you should first look for something to pay tribute to the country, or place and then something about the sport, team or activity, e.g. history of Rotary in Japan, rugby in New Zealand, or education systems in the Soviet Union. The aim is to show your visitors that you have thought it worthwhile to put in the work to find out something about their country. The best starting place is to go to the local library reference section and ask the librarian for help. Capital city reference libraries have phone information services which can also help.

Encyclopedias can yield basic information on most countries but remember that they are inevitably at least two years out of date. If you have plans to make references to recent events in the country then it might be a good idea to contact either their embassy or the nearest consulate.

SPEAKING AT

PUBLIC

MEETINGS

Once the main forums for public speaking were social occasions. Now a citizen is quite likely to find that the first time they stand up to talk to a group of people may well be at a public gathering. The occasion may be a protest meeting about a building development, the closing of a street, budget allocations by schools' Parents and Teachers Associations, a parkland conservation proposal, talking to a council sub-committee, or perhaps a local historical society meeting. Whatever the meeting is about it will fall into one of two categories: either *ad hoc* or formal. The *ad hoc* meeting could be a gathering of residents of a particular street to draft a protest about a freeway development. At such a meeting they will often select a delegation to approach a council or a local member of Parliament.

Then there is the meeting of a formally constituted organisation e.g. a Progress Association or maybe a Preservation Society. These have a membership, a written constitution, and office bearers. To a novice speaker it is easy to be confused by the veterans. They know all about something called the Rules of Debate. People jump up and down shouting "point of order" and moving that the motion be "put" as well as foreshadowing amendments. The 'second amendment' for example may be calmly invoked without explanation and can become a mysterious matter for dispute. Just ask what the amendment said. The rules of debate are merely a matter for commonsense. However, you are not expected to know this and a newcomer does not need to know every last enactment of the committee to be allowed to participate.

The basic rules of any meeting for debate are:

1. The meeting is presided over by a Chairperson/President of the organisation or their deputy. At an ad hoc meeting the Chair is usually accepted by consensus. If there is to be a contest, a third party should take the chair and a show of hands be called for.

2. Some organisations demand written notices of motion, others allow them to be brought forward under General Business. A Chair can call for general discussion before motions, but it is the right of anyone to ask for a motion to be accepted. The same discretion applies in *ad hoc* meetings. Of course no notice of motion is required for an *ad hoc* meeting.

3. A motion must have a mover and a seconder. Sometimes where there has been general discussion a speaker will propose a motion, making it up as he or she goes along. However it is wise to put it in a written form as quickly as possible. The mover must speak to the motion, but the seconder can reserve their right to speak later.

4. After the mover or seconder has spoken the chairman should call for speakers against and for the motion, alternatively.

5. Any speaker can move an amendment, which is a

modification of the motion, however it cannot be a direct negative. The amender must have a seconder. The Chair asks the mover of the original motion if they accept the amendment and if they agree, the two propositions merged become the motion.

6. Anyone else at the meeting can put forward another amendment called a Foreshadowed Amendment. It too can be accepted and become the motion.

7. Any member of the gathering can take what is called a 'Point of Order' if the speaker has strayed on to matter not relevant to the motion. An example of this would be if during a motion opposing a freeway, a speaker starts to talk about the standard of bitumen in their street. If, as in that case, the Chair upholds the Point of Order, in effect saying the speaker is wasting time, then the speaker must stop that line. If however, the speaker disagrees with the ruling he can move a motion of dissent from the Chair, who must stand down while his deputy puts the motion. If the meeting does not uphold the Chair then the speaker can continue.

The Point of Order rule is basically sensible and necessary, but as a new speaker you will quickly see that it is much abused. Just the same it is not a good idea for a novice to move dissent unless he or she is very sure the Chairperson has been outrageous.

8. The Chair lets the debate continue until there are no more speakers, unless someone rises and moves that 'the motion be put' which has to be seconded. This closure must then be voted on without delay. If lost, the general debate continues.

9. When the debate is closed the Chair proceeds to put the matters before the meeting in reverse order of their being moved including the changes to the amendment, and finally the motion — if the amendment is passed it becomes a motion.

10. The only other point that a novice needs to know is that even though in some organisations notice of motion should be given, suspense of standing orders can be moved which, if successful, enables a new motion to be brought forward. Some organisations have limited debating time so suspension of standing orders has to be voted on at the meeting to allow the debate to continue beyond closing time.

At first reading, all of the above might appear complicated, but remember the rules of debate are basically commonsense.

General Preparation

1. The venues of the majority of public meetings are usually not very satisfactory for speakers. Either they take place in the open air or else in draughty, dusty halls. There is not much you can do about it. Where public speaking facilities exist they are often old fashioned stand-up microphones. Look closely at the microphone while other people are speaking and calculate whether you will have to raise or lower it for your own use. Assuming there is no microphone you will have to be ready to raise your voice, more than ever the principle of move-your-lips applies. Some small organisations meet

around tables in private rooms and there the reverse applies. Don't raise your voice, be conversational.

2. Make sure you've got your facts right.

(i) If it's a building development approval get a copy and read it, don't rely on what somebody else has told you. Write it out a couple of times to get it clear in your memory. Find any local displays in the shopping centre, council chambers or public library. If there are no public displays, go to the Planning Department and ask them to show you the map of the proposal. It's your right. If it's the case of a Parents and Citizens budgetary allocation and you haven't got a notice paper ring up the Treasurer and ask him or her politely for the income and expenditure figures, in particular the item in which you are interested. It may be that money is being spent on sports uniforms whereas you think it should go on a computer. After you have got those figures ring a couple of computer companies and ask what your proposal might cost. You need this kind of information. It's just not good enough to say you would like to see more money spent on computers. You have to have some estimate of what the cost will be. Otherwise you risk being asked questions which leave you looking stupid.

(ii) Write out your case briefly. This is not necessarily to enable you to read it out verbatim but to fix it in your memory. If you will feel happier, put down your key points on cards. You can read a text, but this is much more difficult at a public meeting than social function.

3. Talk over your material with a neighbour or a friend, preferably someone who is involved. They may have other points to add which you have not thought of.

4. Check the parking and make sure that you get to the venue in plenty of time. If it is an important meeting it may be crowded so be early. Find a seat in the centre and towards the front of the hall, so that you can catch the speaker's eye.

Organisations

Parents and Citizens &
Parents and Friends

As these organisations begin to play an increasing role in school financing, debates about priorities are coming to assume more importance. There may be questions of library expenditure, provision of computer and printer facilities or more gymnasium equipment, to be debated. Sometimes there will be no separate debate on policy which instead will be tested on each line of the budgetary allocations. If you as a public speaker are to make an important and hopefully vote-changing contribution you should make sure that you do the preliminary work along the Preparation section at the start of this book. In this kind of debate comparisons and quotes from the manufacturers and distributors as well as comments by specialists on the efficacy of the proposal are important. What are other comparable schools doing? Ring your relatives and friends with children at other schools.

In seeking prices stop and think laterally for a moment. If for example, you are on the side of computers, find a statement from some authority for the necessity for children to be equipped for the complexities of the modern world so that they can get jobs. Ring the Public Affairs section of major computer companies and ask them for a suitable quote from an educational authority (not a quote from one of their executives). If you are on the side of the Library ring your local library to find out the latest literacy figures and as well the employment exchange to get a quote from someone on how reading and literacy skills are necessary for jobs. If you favour the gymnasium, set out to marshal arguments for physical fitness. Ring the Department of Health and ask for figures on juvenile obesity. Ask for any date they may have on the importance of exercise for children of school age. Ask them to supply a quote from one health authority.

These same guidelines apply to all public speaking when you want to win a case in any organisation, be it school, tennis club or city council. The speech should be based on:

1. Working out precisely what you want to achieve.
2. Research to find supporting statistical material and facts. Where expenditure is involved you must have a credible estimate.

The Meeting

1. When you arrive check if there is a book where speakers have to put their names down.
2. When the occasion comes for you to speak raise your right hand above your head with the index finger stretched or holding an agenda sheet. In a normal meeting there is no need to stand up and wave desper-

ately as if you are farewelling someone on a cruise ship. If the Chair selects someone ahead of you try to establish eye contact accompanied by a polite gesture to remind him that you wish to be next.

3. When moving say "Mr Chair/Madam Chair, I wish to move a motion in the following terms which I have written out (if applicable)" OR "I wish to speak in favour of the motion/amendment/foreshadowed amendment".

4. After that introductory sentence go straight into your argument, because getting your argument across is the priority. Only after that do you move to counter other arguments.

5. Use your quote at the end of your speech, e.g. "I have spoken about the need for the pursuit of physical fitness at a young age. Let me quote just one prominent authority on children's health ..."

6. Conclude by repeating where you stand and a short key sentence of your argument, e.g. "I support the motion that our children's health and futures are at stake."

7. If a Point of Order is made against you by someone, don't argue, look to the Chairperson. If he or she rules against you, almost always accept it, unless it is outrageous and there is vocal feeling from the audience. Dissent from the ruling of the Chair often exasperates members of the audience, even though they might accept the speaker's basic stand.

8. If someone interjects during your speech, keep talking and if they persist appeal to the Chair, firmly. You

need to be an experienced speaker to cut off interruptions and unless you handle them with wit and good humour your put down may backfire against you.

For some people the chance to speak at a public meeting may come up only once in a lifetime such as when the council tries to put a rubbish tip at the bottom of your garden. For others the first speech at the Parents and Citizens may be the start of a long and rewarding participation in public service.

After you have spoken a few times in public you will start to develop a sense of feeling about the meeting which in turn enables you to rework your arguments on your feet. To be able to do this is, in its own way, as much a pleasure as that gained by the social speaker from having people laughing at his jokes.

This section has not attempted to lay down guidelines for political meetings for the simple reason that speakers in the jungle of party politics have to learn from experience, with a little help from their friends. The basic rules of debate as outlined above should still apply in political meetings, but alas they often don't. Every meeting is a learning process.

BUSINESS

SPEAKING

There are thousands of books on the art of selling, some good, some not so good. Beyond the basic rules, the varieties of sales techniques are as infinite as the products of the world. Selling is not the subject of this section, except to be frank at one remove. It is true that anything that is good for the image of the company is ultimately good for its sales. Increasingly today business people find that they are being called upon to play public speaking roles. There are three broad categories of business public speaking:

1. The social function

    This may involve an after dinner speech to a local, state or national group; the luncheon address to a service club; the presentation of awards either sponsored by the company or to be presented by you as a guest of an institution. It may also involve the acceptance of awards.

2. The convention speech

    This may be to an industry association; a commercially promoted convention or to government sponsored meetings, e.g. the difficulties of drug evaluations in the future. Again while these have a direct effect on sales and the company's image, they are not 'selling' speeches.

3. The public relations speech

    Increasingly these days you will be asked to speak on a debated issue. This may be at a group as small as a school, service club, or as large as a local government conference. Often the speaker has to present a case for his/her industry or company in a forum where there will be criticism and opposition: conservation issues are very common and they will continue to grow in importance. Business has to be able to put its case and the tone in which the case is put, will often be as important as the research.

Speaking After Business Functions

The speech given after dinner or lunch follows the same broad guidelines as social public speaking. Preparation on the venue is set out earlier in this book. If you can't check out these points, delegate them, or ask the people who invited you to help with the answers. For you it's just as important to get the venue right as it is for the best man at a wedding.

Essential Research

1. The names of the club officers and brief background.
2. Basic history of the organisation, when it was founded and how many members it has.
3. Is it part of a world-wide movement, e.g. Rotary or Amnesty International, to which some tribute or acknowledgement should be paid?
4. Explain who you are and where you are coming from as briefly as possible. Something about your personal background in relation to your job, modestly put, should suffice.
5. Jokes.

The Speech

The accepted length is fifteen to twenty minutes. It should include:

1. Thanks to those who invited you.

2. An appropriate quote about the organisation, its history etc. or if you have been asked to speak about your industry and company, first tell them something personal about yourself. That you are married, have two children and collect postage stamps or old car number plates or whatever. This humanises you. Remember, this audience is neutral and not necessarily friendly and supportive as at a wedding or christening. Then say something about the industry and your company. Stress the benefits to the community and of employment. Explain how many jobs outside the company are created by each person employed by your company. Give export earnings.

3. Where it is an award presentation, speeches are usually shorter, five to ten minutes. Apart from the winner, prominent people should be welcomed and the judges should be thanked. There should be a few words about the background of the award and then some comments from the judges on why they have selected the recipient. Finally there is the presentation.

4. Where you are receiving an award the organisers donors and/or sponsors should be thanked as well as the judges. There should be a reference to others in your company or industry involved in making the product.

Conventions

At a convention, you are only one among a number of speakers and comparisons may well be made of your performance with other speakers. This is not an occasion for speaking off the top of your head, however good you are at the in-company sales convention. Therefore careful presentation is essential.

Conventions require prepared, written text if you are to be a success. As well many major convention organisers like a text in advance so that it can be circulated at the end of your speech. All the venue checks as laid out in pages 19-22 should be carried out on your behalf or the information supplied by the organiser.

The usual convention speech including questions lasts for about one hour, although it is sometimes half an hour. If question time is allocated it is usually ten minutes so the speaker must plan to speak to length. There is nothing more embarrassing than for a speaker to sit down too soon leaving an unprepared chairperson to take up the slack. Sometimes speakers are asked to be part of a panel discussion, which could be either autonomous or the follow-up from another speaker. If you have not had any experience in doing hour long speeches you'll be surprised how long it takes. Set yourself a deadline of say a week in advance of when the paper is due, or when it is to be sent to the organisers.

Any convention will have a podium, so you have to make a decision on whether to shift the pages to the side or to pin. (See Preparation page 26.) For a long speech, the best course is to put the pages aside, rather than pinning them and turning over. Make sure you have the pages clearly numbered. Again don't use clips as they slip. Always have a watch with you to help you keep to time. There may be a clock somewhere in the auditorium, but they're often badly placed for speakers, way down the back of the hall, or at the side, or even behind you.

A glass of water is necessary not only as a prop, if you want to pause, but also in recognition of the fact that talking for an hour can be dry work. The notorious trick of judges of putting some gin in the water carafe is not a good idea in the more testing arena of a convention. You are going to have to talk for some time, not just indulge in witty asides. Before starting, remember to clean your reading glasses as lighting is often appalling in convention halls. It is also wise to avoid reading from glossy paper as there may well be an irritating reflection from the gloss surface.

The Speech

1. Thank the person who introduced you, but it is not necessary to thank the organisers or promoters.

2. Announce your topic again as this will give people time to settle. An apposite quote from a good authority

provides an attention-getting opening.

3. Then a brief summary of your theme before moving into the main body of the speech. Most conventions are too solemn and a few jokes are often a pleasant relief. But they should come from the subject matter and avoid being too much of a private joke known only to a few colleagues. Test it out on a friend. Don't rush the joke into the speech. Signal it with some phrase like: 'A traditional joke in the thermo-plastic industry underlines the point I am seeking to make.'

6. The wind-up. Put all your arguments together for a summary. Indicate to the audience that the end is at hand, with some phrase like 'in conclusion.' If you are taking part in a forum the wind-up can be a trap, unless you have marshalled just what you want to say as you would for a longer speech. You have to be prepared for the possibility that one of the other participants may dry up after making too brief a contribution, leaving you to reiterate the points made earlier.

Public Relations Speaking

Public relations speaking is usually when you have to go into an outside forum and talk about your company's or your industry's policies. Such tasks are no longer confined to top management and increasingly more and more middle-ranking executives are being asked to speak in public. It is true that some business people hark back to the good old days when they never had to explain themselves. That's all very well but now business is seen to be in another market place, apart from that place where it sells its wares.

The same procedures for basic preparation as laid out at the beginning of the book apply.

When it comes to research, the first aim is to know your opposition. You might read the arguments against your company's planned new office or factory and be so annoyed by them, as to think that they're not worth refuting. However, that is a luxury you cannot afford.

Research

1. Read the critics. Your company's corporate affairs unit or library should have material. If you are a small, or medium sized company, go to your industry association. Another possible source is a reputable press

cutting service, who will, for a fee, provide you will a cross section of news, opinion about your industry.

2. Then prepare your own case using the same sources. Your state reference library has resource reading lists on many controversial topics.

Let us look at a hypothetical example and how research can help you win your case. A weed-spray, Dandelion-Ded, distributed by your company has been accused of affecting the respiratory tracts of small dogs. Their weakened lungs then make them vulnerable to various diseases, some fatal. It is claimed that in America a number of states have banned Dandelion-Ded under another name.

Your company has been asked by the Chihuahua Breeders Association whether it has anything to say because the annual meeting coming up has a motion before it asking governments to ban Dandelion-Ded. You've been nominated to answer the query. Your state sales manager says that reps have been reporting that hardware and pet stores have been cutting back on Dandelion-Ded orders.

1. Check the opposition. Your industry association has one press cutting from a pug-breeder in the mountains. She states that in the past fortnight she has lost eight dogs from sudden chest diseases and the only explanation she can find is Dandelion-Ded, which she had been using over the past year. You order a copy of the Chihuahua Breeders Association journal and find that all that has been done is to reproduce without comment, the newspaper article. You ring the woman breeder. She read about it in an overseas dog journal, she says.

2. Your side. All the industry association has is that sole press cutting. You fax your affiliate in Boston for information as well as asking whether the complaints were in the wintertime as you suspect that winter in the mountains may have had as much to do with the dogs' deaths, as any pesticide. Boston replies with a report of one case in Maine of a breeder who last December went bankrupt and a month later blamed Dandelion-Ded and announced her intention to sue. She named a veterinary surgeon, who had supported her diagnosis. However, when Boston had contacted the surgeon he denied it: they had died of pneumonia. The threatened legal action had not eventuated. But the allegation was reported on several television stations at the time. There is an independent veterinary opinion refuting the claim. So you can go to the breeders' meeting with a convincing speech, but to put it together required research and tracing the allegation back to its source. That is the whole basis of good business public relations speaking. It is not enough to go along and depend on the veterinary opinions. You have to take the argument of the other side.

GREAT

SPEECHES

Delivering a speech is one of the most effective ways of influencing people. Speech is magic. It has sent armies to war. It has overthrown tyrants. It has won the hearts of women. The rise of the printed word has not diminished the power of oration nor has the development of radio and television in the latter half of this century. You only have to look at any recent election campaign involving huge outdoor rallies or live television debates to realise that the power of speech continues to increase.

Oration is an art. It is not enough to simply state the obvious. A speaker must elaborate and convince. As the Roman orator Cicero pointed out "If truth were self-evident, eloquence would not be necessary." A good speaker must appeal to an audience on many different levels: emotional, economic, political or otherwise. A speech must inspire, persuade, calm or unify.

There are many things to consider when writing and delivering a speech but one of the most important would have to be the first and last sentences. Clear and striking opening remarks that grab the audience's attention are essential while a powerful last phrase that hovers in the air after you sit down will make sure that the main thrust of your speech is remembered. All four great speeches included in this chapter are excellent examples of memorable opening lines and dramatic endings.

The four speeches included here are only a few of the many speeches that have changed the course of history. Just consider some of the orators who have stirred crowds or even nations: Mahatma Ghandi, Fidel Castro, Adolf Hitler, Benito Mussolini, Franklin D. Roosevelt, Sir Winston Churchill, John F. Kennedy, Vladimir Lenin, General de Gaulle, Leon Trotsky, Margaret Thatcher, Archbishop Desmond Tutu, Nelson Mandela, Martin Luther King Jnr., Eva Peron and Cory Aquino.

Included in this chapter are great moments from some of the most mighty orators of recent times. Why have they received so much acclaim? What made their speeches so memorable? Why do high school students study the Gettysburg Address by Abraham Lincoln, for example, when it was not even particularly well received at the time of its delivery? What makes a masterpiece? What techniques are used? You may not be able to glean a blueprint for successful public speaking from these great orators but studying their techniques will at least put you on the right track.

The Gettysburg Address

The Gettysburg Address, delivered by Abraham Lincoln on 19 November, 1863, remains one of the finest recorded speeches of modern times. The occasion took place after one of the most decisive battles in the American Civil War, the Battle of Gettysburg, had been won by the Army of the Potomac, at a great loss of life to both sides. A prominent Gettysburg citizen suggested that some ground be set aside in the middle of the battlefield for a national war cemetery.

The Honourable Edward Everett of Massachusetts, considered one of the country's finest speechmakers, was invited to dedicate it. That Abraham Lincoln was asked to say "a few appropriate remarks" after Everett's speech was almost an afterthought. Some believed the young Illinois attorney would not be able to manage a suitable speech for such a grave occasion. After some deliberation, a formal invitation was finally sent to Lincoln, nearly six weeks after Everett had been asked to speak.

It arrived two weeks before the event. With so little time Lincoln prepared most of the speech on the journey to Gettysburg. Yet in that short time Lincoln crafted the masterpiece that appears in full on the next page.

Fourscore and seven years ago our fathers brought forth on this continent a new nation, conceived in liberty, and dedicated to the proposition that all men are created equal.

Now we are engaged in a great civil war, testing whether that nation, or any nation so conceived and so dedicated, can long endure. We are met on a great battlefield of that war. We have come to dedicate a portion of that field as a final resting-place for those who here gave their lives that that nation might live. It is altogether fitting and proper that we should do this.

But in a larger sense, we cannot dedicate — we cannot consecrate — we cannot hallow — his ground. The brave men, living and dead, who struggled here, have consecrated it far above our poor power to add or detract. The world will little note nor long remember what we say here, but it can never forget what they did here. It is for us, the living, rather, to be dedicated here to the unfinished work which they who fought here have thus far so nobly advanced. It is rather for us to be here dedicated to the great task remaining before us — that from these honoured dead we take increased devotion to that cause for which they gave the last full measure of devotion; that we here highly resolve that these dead shall not have died in vain; that this nation, under God, shall have a new birth of freedom; and that government of the people, by the people, for the people, shall not perish from the earth.

President Lincoln spoke in a loud, clear voice as the speech was long before the advent of microphones. The reaction to the address was lukewarm, however. Some felt it was over before it had begun. Applause was slow and perfunctory. Some newspapers ridiculed the speech, only a few praised it and scarcely a handful of people recognised it for the masterpiece that it was.

Ironically, Edward Everett was one of the few to give it due praise. He wrote to Lincoln "I should be glad if I could flatter myself that I came as near the central idea of the occasion in two hours as you did in two minutes." Lincoln replied: "You could not have been excused to make a short address, nor I a long one. I am pleased to know that, in your judgment, the little I did say was not entirely a failure."

Why is the address considered so outstanding? Like the other four great speeches included in this chapter, the opening line has been indelibly etched upon popular memory. Lincoln chose to spell out the years in such a way that the audience could actually envisage the passing of time. "Fourscore] and seven years ago" has a timeless and epic appeal. There would have been no impact if he had begun: "87 years ago, our fathers...".

Lincoln also observed two golden rules of speechmaking: brevity and simple language. While Everett's speech used the high-flowing vernacular of the time, Lincoln's simply constructed sentences could be interpreted in a thousand different ways. In this way he managed to paint a bigger picture — that where there was freedom or democracy people had fought for it and that it was worth loss of life. His speech also unified the crowd because it rose above laying blame on either side and concentrated on the higher ideal of democracy.

Sir Winston Churchill

Churchill is considered one of the greatest orators of modern times, yet he was once terrified of giving speeches. During his second address to Parliament he actually collapsed from nervous anxiety! He felt inferior because he lacked a university education and was handicapped by a lisp in his youth which made him the object of ridicule. In fact a surgeon he once visited for medical advice advised him never to undertake an occupation where speaking was a necessary part of making a living. Yet Churchill rose to become one of the most powerful men in the world during World War II and is considered among the best speechmakers of this century.

Winston Churchill developed a formula for successful speeches. He realised that it was far more important for speeches to *sound* good, than to *read* well. As radio was the most immediate mass communication medium of the time, he wrote his speeches for the ear not for the eye. He also believed that a speech should have the natural rhythm of conversation so that if the listener did not catch everything he was saying due to bad reception or some other distraction, he or she would still get the gist of it.

Churchill developed five basic principles for writing

speeches. If you follow these you will have written a fine speech. They are:

1. strong opening

2. one main theme

3. simple language

4. use of analogy

5. emotional ending

One of Churchill's best-known speeches was as the new British Prime Minister on 13 May, 1940 in the House of Commons. At the time, Britain was in a despondent and despairing mood as World War II looked like it would go on forever. Part of this momentous speech is reproduced below.

...We are in the preliminary stage of one of the greatest battles in history...In this crisis I hope I may be pardoned if I do not address the House at any length today. I hope that any of my friends and colleagues, or former colleagues, who are affected by the political reconstruction, will make all allowance for any lack of ceremony with which it has been necessary to act. I would say to the House, as I said to those who have joined this Government: "I have nothing to offer but blood, toil, tears and sweat."

We have before us an ordeal of the most grievous kind. We have before us many, many long months of struggle and of suffering. You ask what is our policy? I will say: It is to wage war, by sea, land and air, with all our might and with all the strength that God can give us: to wage war against a monstrous tyranny, never surpassed in the dark, lamentable catalogue of human crime. That is our policy. You ask, What is our aim? I can answer in one word: Victory — victory at all costs, victory in spite of all terror, victory, however long and hard the road may be; for without victory, there is no survival. Let that be realised; no survival for the British Empire; no survival for all that the British Empire has stood for, no survival for the urge and impulse of the ages, that mankind will move forward towards its goal. But I take up my task with buoyancy and hope. I feel sure that our cause will not be suffered to fail among men. At this time I feel entitled to claim the aid of all, and I say, "Come, then, let us go forward together with our united strength.

Churchill later said of the speech: "In all our long history no Prime Minister had ever been able to present to Parliament and the nation a programme at once so short and so popular."

The success of Churchill's speech lies, like Lincoln's, in its brevity and simple structure. It also uses the old device of repetition very effectively. "Victory" and "survival" are the keywords in this speech. Here they are almost chant-like and their use is inspired. National morale was at an all-time low. Britain needed something to hope for, some sign of optimism in all the darkness. Churchill did not disappoint them. His speech was tremendously uplifting and well-timed. For the first time Britain could see a light at the end of the tunnel, so to speak. It is a perfect example of what public speaking experts call 'knowing your audience'. Churchill accurately gauged the national mood and told the British people what they longed to hear.

Churchill also makes good use of the rhetorical question. Some speechwriters abuse this but the device is used extremely well here. He asks in closing "What is our policy?" and "What is our aim?" These questions quicken the pace of the speech, becoming rousing cries which build up to a dramatic ending. Churchill once suggested that you should write the last part of your speech first so that you know where you are headed at the beginning. This is not as silly as it sounds. You should never begin writing a speech unless you know what you want the audience to do when it is finished. Ask yourself: What is the bottom line? How do you want the audience to react? In this instance Churchill wanted unity and support. To achieve this he ended his speech with one of his favourite devices — an emotional appeal. His extols the virtues of the British Empire and calls for unity, thereby pulling at the national heartstrings.

Churchill made many more rousing speeches. Another well-known occasion was his address on 4 June, 1940, following the Battle of Dunkirk, a decisive World War II battle in which the German army inflicted a significant defeat on the British. The purpose of this speech was to remind the nation and its allies why they were fighting and to express confidence in their ultimate victory. The ending is a classic example of rousing the audience by having a dramatic and emotional ending.

...We shall go on to the end, we shall fight in France, we shall fight on the seas and oceans, we shall fight with growing confidence and growing strength in the air, we shall defend our island, whatever the cost may be, we shall

fight on the beaches, we shall fight on the landing grounds, we shall fight in the fields and in the streets, we shall fight in the hills; we shall never surrender...

Amazingly the British people came to believe that the Battle of Dunkirk (one of the British Army's most ignominious defeats) was in fact a victory.

It often happened in Churchill's speeches during World War II that phrases passed into history as soon as they were spoken. On 18 June, 1940, when the German airforce was regularly bombing Britain, he made another rousing speech. The morale of the nation was gradually sinking and Churchill resolved to give encouragement. The end of his speech may have borrowed something from Shakespeare as it, too, ended dramatically.

Let us therefore brace ourselves to our duties, and so bear ourselves that, if the British Empire and its Commonwealth last for a thousand years, men will say, "This was their finest hour."

Martin Luther King

That the 1960s was a decade of political upheaval and change goes without saying. Nowhere was this more apparent than in the United States, where the civil rights movement was gaining momentum, triggered by the centenary celebration of the American Civil War in 1961. Political protest came to the boil in 1963. It was the centenary of President Lincoln's Emancipation Proclamation yet black Americans were still just as oppressed by institutionalised racism as they had been by slavery. Protests and demonstrations attracted people in their thousands and world attention focused on the black struggle. One black leader suggested a march on Washington. Many thought the divided black American community could never unite for such a demonstration, yet between 200,000 and 250,000 did march on Washington on 28 August, 1963.

The climax of the rally was a speech given by Reverend Martin Luther King, Jr., of the Southern Christian Leadership. King had become a high profile leader of the black movement, adopting Ghandi's stance of 'nonresistance'. The march on Washington went off without any violence and received unanimous praise. In October, 1964, Reverend Martin Luther King, Jr., was awarded the Nobel Peace Prize as a fitting reward for his efforts.

At 32, he was the youngest man ever to receive the prestigious prize. Tragically, he was assassinated four years later in Memphis, Tennessee.

An excerpt from his speech on that momentous day in 1963 is reproduced below. The entire speech is too long to include in this book but we have selected the most well-known part for analysis. Up until this point Martin Luther King, Jr. had followed all the golden rules of speechmaking. After a strong opening, he launches straight into his main theme — freedom. In expanding this theme, he makes frequent use of analogy, referring to the Constitution and the Declaration of Independence as a cheque which had bounced on black people; they had come to the capital to cash this cheque.

The phrase "I have a dream", which is where we take up his speech, signals the end of his examination of the present situation of Negroes and introduces his hopes for the future. He repeats this often throughout the speech and the repetition is uplifting.

...I say to you today, my friends, even though we face the difficulties of today and tomorrow, I still have a dream. It is a dream deeply rooted in the American dream. I have a dream that one day this Nation will rise up and live out the true meaning of its creeds — "we hold these truths to be self-evident that all men are created equal."

I have a dream that one day on the red hills of Georgia the sons of slaves and the sons of former slaveowners will be able to sit down together at the table of brotherhood. I have a dream that one day even the state of Mississippi, sweltering with the heat of injustice, sweltering with the heat of oppression, will be transformed into an oasis of freedom and justice.

I have a dream that my four little children will one day live in a nation where they will not be judged by the colour of their skin but by the content of their character.

I have a dream today.

I have a dream that one day the state of Alabama, whose governor's lips are presently dripping with the words of interposition and nullification, will be transformed into a situation where little black boys and black girls will be able to join hands with little white boys and white girls and walk together as sisters and brothers.

I have a dream today.

I have a dream that one day every valley shall be exalted, every hill and mountain shall be made low, the rough places will be made plain, and the crooked places will be made straight, and the glory of the Lord shall be revealed, and all flesh shall see it together.

This is our hope. This is the faith with which I return to the South. With this faith we will be able to hew out of the mountain of despair a stone of hope. With this faith we will be able to transform the jangling discords of our nation into a beautiful symphony of brotherhood. With this faith we will be able to work together, to pray together, to struggle together, to go to jail together, to stand up for freedom together, knowing that we will be free one day.

This will be the day when all of God's children will be able to sing with new meaning 'My country 'tis of thee, sweet land of liberty, of thee I sing. Land where my fathers died, land of the pilgrim's pride, from every mountainside, let freedom ring.'

And if America is to be a great nation this must become true. So let freedom ring from the prodigious hilltops of New Hampshire! Let freedom ring from the mighty mountains of New York! Let freedom ring from the heightening Alleghenies of Pennsylvania!

Let freedom ring from the snowcapped Rockies of Colorado!

Let freedom ring from the curvaceous peaks of California!

But not only that; let freedom ring from Stone Mountain of Georgia!

Let freedom ring from every hill and mole hill of Mississippi. From every mountainside, let freedom ring. When we let freedom ring, when we let it ring from every village and every hamlet from every state and every city, we will be able to speed up that day when all of God's children, black men and white men, Jews and Gentiles, Protestants and Catholics, will be able to join hands and sing in the words of that old Negro spiritual, 'Free at last! Free at last! Thank God almighty, we are free at last.'

* Reprinted, by kind permission of George Allen & Unwin Ltd, from *What Manner of Man: a Biography of Martin Luther King* by L. Bennett.

All Churchill's five principles of speechmaking can be found in this oration. Martin Luther King's opening remarks are inspired: "I am happy to join with you today in what will go down in history as the greatest demonstration for freedom in the history of the Nation." (1). One main theme, freedom for black people, is introduced and adhered to throughout the speech (2). Everyday phrases give the speech a conversational tone while (3) repetition is constantly used to drive the main message home. (4) Frequent use is made of analogy. Mississippi, notorious for long hot summers and some of the country's worst racism, is likened to a desert 'sweltering with the heat of injustice, sweltering with the heat of oppression'. (5) The close of the speech is an exemplary use of dramatic ending: "Thank God Almighty, we are free at last!"

However, it is King's constant repetition of key phrases such as 'with this faith' and 'let freedom ring' throughout the speech which makes it so strong. The device is used everywhere and yet it is not overused. Earlier on, he keeps saying 'we can never be satisfied' and 'now is the time'. Instead of sounding false and unnatural this use of repetition simply adds emphasis and slowly builds up to the climax.

Mark Antony in *Julius Caesar*

Probably no opening remarks are as well-known or have been as oft-quoted as the first line of Mark Antony's speech in Shakespeare's *Julius Caesar:* "Friends, Romans, countrymen, lend me your ears;". Humorous variations such as "Friends, Romans, countrymen, put down your beers" abound. On one memorable occasion the second line fell victim to the speaker's wit as well. A meeting of winemakers concerned with a threatened increase in liquor tax invited the government's Treasurer, named Berry, to speak. He was introduced with the words "Friends, Romans, countrymen, put down your beers. We have come to seize Berry, not to praise him!"

Mark Antony makes his speech under difficult circumstances in the play. Caesar has just been assassinated by trusted colleagues led by Cassius and Brutus. Antony arrives just after the slaying and pretends to be swayed by their arguments justifying the killing but is secretly plotting revenge. He asks to deliver the funeral oration, knowing how easily a crowd can be swayed by a skilful speaker and they reluctantly agree. This move proves to be their downfall. Brutus speaks first, delivering an earnest and carefully worded speech to justify the assassination and then hands over to Mark Antony. Antony is a brilliant orator and politician. Although he faces a hostile crowd unwilling to hear any good about Caesar, his speech is a masterpiece of emotional manipulation which turns the mob against the conspirators. It is a passionate appeal in stark contrast to Brutus's prosaic appeal to reason.

His opening line is effective in silencing the crowd; he also places himself on their level by calling them "friends". But it is mainly the use of repetition which makes his speech so successful. This is a perfect example of knowing what you want from an audience before you begin. Mark Antony wants the crowd to support him in his revenge and he gets what he wants. At the beginning of the speech he feels his way with the audience, appealing to their grief and even crying himself. Once he has won them over to his side he whips them up into hysteria.

He begins by saying that "Brutus is an honourable man" and continually repeats this until, little by little, the mob refuse to believe it. Their rage grows as Antony winds up his speech. By the end they are crying "Revenge!" "Slay!" and charge out in search of the assassins. The seeds of civil war have been planted and the decline of the Roman Empire begins. The speech is reproduced below. When reading the speech remember that Antony frequently paused at the end of a sentence to add emphasis.

Friends, Romans, countrymen, lend me your ears;
I come to bury Caesar, not to praise him.
The evil that men do lives after them;
The good is oft interred with their bones;
So let it be with Caesar. The noble Brutus
Hath told you Caesar was ambitious:

If it were so, it was a grievous fault;
And grievously hath Caesar answer'd it.
Here, under leave of Brutus and the rest,
(For Brutus is an honourable man;
So are they all, all honourable men;)
Come I to speak in Caesar's funeral.
He was my friend, faithful and just to me:
But Brutus says he was ambitious;
And Brutus is an honourable man.
He hath brought many captives home to Rome,
Whose ransoms did the general coffers fill:
Did this in Caesar seem ambitious?
When that the poor have cried, Caesar hath wept;
Ambition should be made of sterner stuff:
Yet Brutus says he was ambitious;
And Brutus is an honourable man.
You all did see that on the Lupercal
I thrice presented him with a kingly crown,
Which he did thrice refuse. Was this ambition?
Yet Brutus says he was ambitious;
And, sure, he is an honourable man.
I speak not to disprove what Brutus spoke,
But here I am to speak what I do know.
You all did love him once, — not without cause;
What cause withholds you, then, to mourn for him?
O judgment, thou art fled to brutish beasts,
And men have lost their reason! — Bear with me:
My heart is in the coffin there with Caesar,
And I must pause till it come back to me.

There are many other openings from Shakespeare's speeches and soliloquies which have also become famous. "To be or not to be, — that is the question:" from *Hamlet,*

Prince of Denmark, is another well-known line which has undergone so many changes that it is impossible to list them here. One of the most effective ways of using this line is to quote it accurately or substitute another verb for "be" depending on the occasion.

The Life and Death of King Richard III has also spawned some memorable beginnings. "Now is the winter of our discontent" is much quoted by speechmakers as is "A horse! A horse! my kingdom for a horse! from the same play.

Romeo and Juliet has provided material for speechmakers and comedians alike. So too has "Is this a dagger which I see before me," from *Macbeth*. However, Romeo's lovesick ode to Juliet as she appears at a window in the famous balcony scene is especially popular. This has been used in everything from speeches to advertisements for chocolate bars.

He jests at scars, that never felt a wound.— Juliet appears above, at a window.

But, soft! what light through yonder window breaks!

It is the east, and Juliet is the sun!–

It is important to note that all these four speeches were made by men experienced in public life. For Abraham Lincoln and Winston Churchill their very livelihood depended on their ability to persuade and convince through their powers of oratory. Martin Luther King Jnr. delivered speeches for years from the pulpit before he committed himself to the Black Power movement. Although Mark Antony is a fictional character, the techniques used by Shakespeare in writing this speech are no less useful than the devices of real orators.

USEFUL

QUOTES

Age

The Grecian ladies counted their age from their marriage, not their birth.
Homer

One should never trust a woman who tells one her real age. A woman who would tell one that, would tell one anything.
Oscar Wilde

There are so many ways of us dying it's astonishing any of us choose old age.
Beryl Bainbridge

Old age takes away from us what we have inherited and gives us what we have earned.
Gerald Brenan

The young have aspirations that never come to pass, the old have reminiscences of what never happened.
Saki (H.H. Munro)

It is a terrible thing for an old woman to outlive her dogs.
Camino Real, Tennessee Williams

The older you get, the faster you ran as a kid.
Steve Owen

Most people say that as you get old, you have to give up things. I think you get old because you give up things.
Theodore F. Green

119

Men are like wine. Some turn to vinegar, but the best improve with age.
C.E.M. Joad

Whatever poet, orator, or sage may say of it, old age is still old age.
Henry Wadsworth Longfellow

Art, Music, Film, Theatre

Anyone who paints a sky green and pastures blue ought to be sterilised.
Adolf Hitler

Surely nothing has to listen to so many stupid remarks as a painting in a museum.
Edmónd and Jules de Goncourt

To reveal art and conceal the artist, is art's aim.
The Picture of Dorian Gray, Oscar Wilde

Art is either a plagiarist or a revolutionist.
Paul Gauguin

An artist's career always begins tomorrow.
James McNeill Whistler

Art for art's sake.
English proverb

Art is a jealous mistress.
Wealth, Ralph Waldo Emerson

The true artist will let his wife starve, his children go barefoot, his mother drudge for his living at seventy, sooner than work at anything but his art.
  George Bernard Shaw

Every artist writes his own autobiography.
  The New Spirit, Havelock Ellis

Art is not a pastime but a priesthood.
  Jean Cocteau

Art is a form of catharsis.
  Dorothy Parker

Art is the most intense mode of individualism that the world has known.
  The Soul of Man Under Socialism, Oscar Wilde

I like a film to have a beginning, a middle and an end, but not necessarily in that order.
  Jean-Luc Godard

The cinema is truth 24 times a second.
  Jean-Luc Godard

The cinema is not a slice of life, but a piece of cake.
  Alfred Hitchcock

It's the biggest trainset a boy ever had.
  Orson Wells, on Hollywood

I started at the top and worked my way down.
  Orson Wells

The best films are best because of nobody but the director.
  Roman Polanski

What puzzles most of us are the things that have been left in the movies rather than the things which have been taken out.
Agnes Repplier

Actors are cattle.
Alfred Hitchcock

The physical labour actors have to do wouldn't tax an embryo.
Spencer Tracy

Acting is a bum's life. Quitting acting, that is a sign of maturity.
Marlon Brando

I am the unusual and do not need camera angles.
Charlie Chaplin

She ran the whole gamut of emotions from A to B.
Dorothy Parker on Katherine Hepburn

Long experience has taught me that in England nobody goes to the theatre unless he or she has bronchitis.
Ego.6, James Agate

I don't regard Brecht as a man of iron-grey purpose and intellect, I think he is a theatrical whore of the first quality.
Peter Hall, The Frank Muir Book

I don't know anything about music. In my line you don't have to.
Elvis Presley

I write as a sow pisses.
Mozart

Bach almost persuades me to be a Christian.
Roger Fry

Good music isn't nearly so bad as it sounds.
Harry Zelzer

Wagner has some wonderful moments but awful half hours.
Rossini

The joy of music should never be interrupted by a commercial.
Leonard Bernstein

Classical music is the kind we keep hopin' will turn into a tune.
Kin Hubbard

Music is the only language in which you cannot say a sarcastic thing.
John Erskine

Rock 'n' roll is the most brutal, ugly, vicious form of expression — sly, lewd, in fact plain dirty...
Frank Sinatra, 1957

It is extraordinary how potent cheap music is.
Noel Coward

If music be the food of love, play on;
Twelfth Night, Shakespeare

Music has charms to soothe a savage beast.
The Mourning Bride, William Congreve

The English may not like music — but they absolutely love the noise it makes.
William Beebe, The Wit of Music, L. Ayre

I think popular music is one of the few things in the twentieth century that has made giant strides in reverse.
Bing Crosby

You have Van Gogh's ear for music.
Billy Wilder to Cliff Osmond

Music is the eye of the ear.
 English proverb

Dancing is a perpendicular expression of a horizontal desire.
 George Bernard Shaw

It is not a writer's business to hold opinions.
 William Butler Yeats

Style and structure are the essence of a great book; great ideas
are hogwash.
 Vladimir Nabokov, 1958

An author ought to write for the youth of his own generation,
the critics of the next, and the schoolmasters of ever afterwards.
 F. Scott Fitzgerald

Nobody writes if they had a happy childhood.
 Joseph Hergesheimer

There's no way anybody can sit down and write a best seller.
 Harold Robbins

If a writer has to rob his mother, he will not hesitate; 'Ode to a
Grecian Urn' is worth any number of old ladies.
 William Faulkner

That's not writing, that's typing.
 Truman Capote on Jack Kerouac

The day will come when everyone will be famous for fifteen
minutes.
 Andy Warhol

I would give all my fame for a pot of ale....
 Henry V, Shakespeare

Beauty

A woman who cannot be ugly is not beautiful.
Karl Kraus

Beauty is in the eye of the beholder.
English proverb

Beauty is only skin deep.
English proverb

There is nothing sane about the worship of beauty.
Intentions, Oscar Wilde

The saying that beauty is but skin deep is but a skin deep saying.
John Ruskin

There are no ugly women, only lazy ones.
Helena Rubenstein

The most beautiful make-up of a woman is passion. But cosmetics are easier to buy.
Yves Saint Laurent

The best thing is to look natural, but it takes makeup to look natural.
Calvin Klein

It is better to be beautiful than good. But...it is better to be good than to be ugly.
The Picture of Dorian Gray , Oscar Wilde

What, when drunk, one sees in other women, one sees in Garbo sober.
Kenneth Tynan

I always say that beauty is only sin deep.
Reginald's Choir Treat, Saki (H H. Munro)

Childhood and Parenthood

Children and fools tell the truth.
English proverb

Only those in the last stages of disease could believe that children are true judges of character.
The Orators, W.H. Auden

Anyone who hates children and dogs can't be all bad.
W.C. Fields

Children are natural mimics — they act like their parents in spite of every attempt to teach them good manners.
Anon

I must have been an insufferable child; all children are.
George Bernard Shaw

Children should be seen and not heard.
English proverb

Spare the rod and spoil the child.
English proverb

Children begin by loving their parents; after a time they judge them; rarely, if ever, do they forgive them.
Oscar Wilde

Parents are the very last people who ought to be allowed to have children.
H.E. Bell

Never have children, only grandchildren.
Gore Vidal

She never quite leaves her children at home, even when she doesn't take them along.
Margaret Culkin Banning

I love children. Especially when they cry — for then someone takes them away.
Nancy Mitford

Why can't life's problems hit us when we're seventeen and know everything?
A.C. Jolly

There's nothing wrong with teenagers that reasoning with them won't aggravate.
Anon

A Jewish man with parents alive is a fifteen-year old boy, and will remain a fifteen-year old boy till they die.
Portnoy's Complaint, Philip Roth

My parents were very old world. They come from Brooklyn, which is the heart of the Old World. Their values in life are God and carpeting.
Woody Allen

No woman can shake off her mother. There should be no more mothers, only women.
Too Good to Be True, George Bernard Shaw

Drink

Work is the curse of the drinking class.
Oscar Wilde

If you resolve to give up smoking, drinking and loving, you don't actually live longer: it just seems longer.
Clement Freud

You're not drunk if you can lie on the floor without holding on.
Dean Martin

One more drink and I'd have been under the host.
Dorothy Parker

Wine is constant proof that God loves us and likes to see us happy.
Benjamin Franklin

Wine has two defects: if you add water to it, you ruin it; if you do not add water it ruins you.
Spanish proverb

Forget the house, forget the children, I want custody of the red and access to the port once a month.
Kevin Childs

Wine is the best liquor to wash glasses in.
Jonathan Swift

A meal without wine is like a day without sunshine.
Louis Pasteur

Champagne...is the only wine that lets a woman stay beautiful after she has drunk it.
Madame de Pompadour

Drinking makes such fools of people, and people are such fools to begin with, that it's compounding a felony.
Robert Benchley

When the wine is in, the wit is out.
English proverb

I drink only to make my friends seem interesting.
Don Marquis

Drink because you are happy — and never because you are miserable.
G.K. Chesterton

One cup of wine is good for a woman; two are degrading; three make her wanton; four destroy her sense of shame.
The Talmud

One reason I don't drink is that I want to know when I'm having a good time.
Lady Nancy Astor

This calls for a drink!
Anon

Economy

If all economists were laid end to end, they would not reach a conclusion.
George Bernard Shaw

My problem lies in reconciling my gross habits with my net income.
Errol Flynn

Collecting more taxes than is absolutely necessary is legalised robbery.
Calvin Coolidge, 30th U.S. President

Say nothing of my debts unless you mean to pay them.
English proverb

One million dollars: A sum that may be honestly acquired by putting aside five hundred dollars out of one's salary every week for forty years.
Anon

We are not concerned with the very poor. They are unthinkable, and only to be approached by the statistician or the poet.
Howard's End, E.M. Forster

A fool and his money are soon parted. What I want to know is how they got together in the first place.
Cyril Fletcher

There was a time when a fool and his money were soon parted, but now it happens to everybody.
The Stevenson Wit, Adlai Stevenson

If you would know what the Lord God thinks of money, you have only to look at those to whom He gives it.
Maurice Baring

Hollywood money isn't money. It's congealed snow, melts in your hand, and there you are.
Dorothy Parker

If there's anyone listening to whom I owe money, I'm prepared to forget it if you are.
Errol Flynn

[Commercial television] It's just like having a licence to print your own money.
Lord Thompson of Fleet

Money can't buy friends, but you can get a better class of enemy.
Spike Milligan

Money is better than poverty, if only for financial reasons.
Without Feathers, Woody Allen

Money is like a sixth sense, without which you cannot make a complete use of the other five.
W. Somerset Maugham

The rich are different from us. *(F. Scott Fitzgerald)*
Yes, they have more money. *(Ernest Hemingway)*

You can be young without money but you can't be old without it.
Cat on a Hot Tin Roof, Tennessee Williams

When I was young I thought money was the most important thing in life: now that I am old I know that it is.
Oscar Wilde

If you can count your money then you are not a really rich man.
Paul Getty

The only thing I like about rich people is their money.
   Lady Nancy Astor

Money is like manure. You have to spread it around or it smells.
   Paul Getty

Remember, that time is money.
   Benjamin Franklin

No one would remember the Good Samaritan if he only had good intentions. He had money as well.
   Margaret Thatcher

The greatest waste of money is to keep it.
   Jackie Gleason

Wealth has never been a sufficient source of honour in itself. It must be advertised, and the normal medium is obtrusively expensive goods.
   The Affluent Society, J.K. Galbraith

Wealth is not the fruit of labour but the result of organised, protected robbery.
   Frantz Fanon

Fashion

Fashion is made to be unfashionable.
Coco Chanel

If you've got it, flaunt it.
Anon

The truly fashionable are beyond fashion.
Cecil Beaton

Blue jeans? They should be worn by farm girls milking cows!
Yves Saint Laurent

A woman is as young as her knee.
Mary Quant

Wearing her skirt halfway up the thigh does not give a woman
the advantage.
Coco Chanel

Don't ever wear artistic jewellery; it wrecks a woman's reputation.
Gigi, Collette

I base most of my fashion taste on what doesn't itch.
Gilda Radner

It is only shallow people who do not judge by appearances.
The Picture of Dorian Gray, Oscar Wilde

Style is knowing who you are, what you want to say, and not
giving a damn.
Gore Vidal

Good taste is better than bad taste, but bad taste is better than
no taste.
Arnold Bennett, 1930

Feminism

But if God had wanted us to think with our wombs, why did he give us a brain?

Clare Booth Luce

Whatever women do they must do twice as well as men to be thought half as good. Luckily, this is not difficult.

Charlotte Whitton

All women are Lesbians, except those who don't know it yet.

Dialog on Women's Liberation, Jill Johnson

The average girl would rather have beauty than brains because she knows that the average man can see much better than he can think.

Ladies' Home Journal

Home is the girl's prison and the woman's workhouse.

George Bernard Shaw

Married women are kept women, and they are beginning to find it out.

Other People, Logan Pearsall Smith

Give women the vote and in five years there will be a crushing tax on bachelors.

Man and Superman, George Bernard Shaw

Physically there is nothing to distinguish human society from the farm-yard except that children are more troublesome and costly than chickens and women are not so completely enslaved as farm stock.

Getting Married, George Bernard Shaw

Food, Cooks & Cooking

The way to a man's heart is through his stomach.
Fanny Fern

Tell me what you eat and I will tell you what you are.
Brillat-Savarin

Old people shouldn't eat health foods. They need all the preservatives they can get.
Robert Orben

What happens to the hole when the cheese has gone?
Bertolt Brecht

Gluttony is an emotional escape, a sign something is eating us.
Peter de Vries

I eat merely to put food out of my mind.
N. F. Simpson

Man is the only animal that eats when he is not hungry, drinks when he is not thirsty, and makes love at all seasons.
Anon

Without bread, without wine, love is nothing.
French saying

My wife and I tried to breakfast together, but we had to stop or our marriage would have been wrecked.
Winston Churchill

Cooking is like love. It should be entered into with abandon or not at all.
Harriet van Horne

Vegetarianism is harmless enough, though it is apt to fill a man with wind and righteousness.
Sir Robert Hutchinson

You do not obtain eminence so cheaply as by eating macaroni instead of mutton chops.
George Bernard Shaw

Let them eat cake.
Attributed to Marie Antoinette, although in circulation well before her time

We may find in the long run that tinned food is a deadlier weapon than the machine gun.
George Orwell

Food is a weapon.
Maxim Litvinov

You cannot feed the hungry on statistics.
David Lloyd George

Be content to remember that those who can make omelettes properly can do nothing else.
Hilaire Belloc

Too many cooks spoil the broth.
English proverb

Any cook should be able to run the country.
Vladimir I. Lenin

Food is an important part of a balanced diet.
Fran Lebowitz

History

Historians may lie but history cannot.
George Saintsbury

The only thing we learn from history is that we do not learn.
Earl Warren

It is not the neutrals or the lukewarms who make history.
Adolf Hitler

History repeats itself; historians repeat each other.
Philip Guedalla

History is a set of lies agreed upon.
Napoleon Bonaparte

History is more or less bunk.
Henry Ford

No great man lives in vain. The history of the world is but the biography of great men.
Thomas Carlyle

History is too serious to be left to historians.
Iain Macleod

Anyone can make history; only a great man can write it.
Oscar Wilde

Humanity

A human being: an ingenious assembly of portable plumbing.
   Human Being, Christopher Morley

Human beings were invented by water as a device for transporting itself from one place to another.
   Tom Robbins

Man is the only animal that blushes. Or needs to.
   Mark Twain

Man's inhumanity to man...
   Man Was Made to Mourn, Robert Burns

Man is the missing link between the ape and the human being.
   Anon

Man is an intelligence in servitude to his organs.
   Aldous Huxley

I love mankind — it's people I can't stand.
   Go Fly a Kite, Charlie Brown, Charles M. Schultz

That's one small step for a man, one giant step for mankind.
   Neil Armstrong setting foot on the moon

Knowledge

Strange how much you've got to know before you know how little you know.
   Anon

Not to know is bad; not to wish to know is worse.
   African proverb

If a little knowledge is dangerous, where is the man who has so much to be out of danger?
Thomas Huxley

What you don't know can't hurt you.
English proverb

Knowledge is power.
English proverb

Our knowledge can only be finite, while our ignorance must necessarily be infinite.
Sir Karl Popper

All that we know is, nothing can be known.
Byron

The trouble with people is not that they don't know but that they know so much that ain't so.
Josh Billings

Education is what survives when what has been learnt has been forgotten.
B F. Skinner

Experience is the name everyone gives to their mistakes.
Lady Windermere's Fan, Oscar Wilde

If I had learned education I would not have had time to learn anything else.
Cornelius Vanderbilt

Law

People say law but they mean wealth.
> *Journals, Ralph Waldo Emerson*

A jury consists of twelve persons chosen to decide who has the better lawyer.
> *Robert Frost*

Injustice is relatively easy to bear; it is justice that hurts.
> *H. L. Mencken*

We do not get good laws to restrain bad people. We get good people to restrain bad laws.
> *All Things Considered, G.K. Chesterton*

Laws are like spider's webs: if some poor weak creature comes up against them, it is caught; but a bigger one can break through and get away.
> *Solon*

Laws were made to be broken.
> *Christopher North*

Good men must not obey the laws too well.
> *Ralph Waldo Emerson*

He is always breaking the law. He broke the law when he was born: his parents were not married.
> *Major Barbara, George Bernard Shaw*

One law for the rich and another for the poor.
> *English proverb*

Law makers should not be law breakers.
> *English proverb*

Life

Life is just a bowl of cherries.
Lew Brown

Such is Life!
Great Expectations, Charles Dickens.

Life is like an onion, which one peels crying.
French proverb

Life is a tragedy when seen close-up, but a comedy in long-shot.
Charlie Chaplin

Life is what we make of it, always has been, always will be.
Grandma Moses

Life begins at forty.
W.B. Pitkin

It is not true that life is one damn thing after another — it is one damn thing over and over.
Edna St Vincent Millay

Variety's the very spice of life
That gives it all the flavour.
William Cowper

Human life begins on the other side of despair.
The Flies, Jean-Paul Sartre

Life is like nothing, because it is everything.
William Golding

Life is nothing until it is lived.
Existentialism is a Humanism, Jean-Paul Sartre

Life was a funny thing that happened to me on the way to the grave.
Quentin Crisp

There must be more to life than having everything!
Maurice Sendak

Love

Love is not the dying moan of a distant violin — it is the triumphant twang of a bedspring.
S. J. Perelman

Absence makes the heart grow fonder.
English proverb

Love is only a dirty trick played on us to achieve continuation of the species.
A Writer's Notebook, W. Somerset Maugham

I can understand companionship. I can understand bought sex in the afternoon. I cannot understand the love affair.
Gore Vidal

A man can be happy with a woman as long as he does not love her.
Oscar Wilde

Love, love, love — all the wretched cant of it, masking egotism, lust, masochism, fantasy under a mythology of sentimental postures.
Germaine Greer

Nobody will ever win the Battle of the Sexes. There's just too much fraternising with the enemy.
Henry Kissinger

The fickleness of the women I love is only equalled by the infernal constancy of the women who love me.
The Philanderer, George Bernard Shaw

Men love in haste, but they detest at leisure.
Byron

'Tis better to have loved and lost
Than never to have loved at all.
Alfred, Lord Tennyson

Love is blind.
English proverb

Love makes the world go round.
English proverb

Love at first sight.
English proverb

Woman begins by resisting a man's advances and ends by blocking his retreat.
Oscar Wilde

Marriage

Marriage is a great institution, but I'm not ready for an institution, yet.
Mae West

Marriage is a wonderful invention; but then again, so is a bicycle repair kit.
Billy Connolly

Marriage is not all bed and breakfast.
Reflections, Noel Coward

It should be a very happy marriage — they are both so in love with him.

Irene Thomas

A man in love is incomplete until he is married. Then he is finished.

Zsa Zsa Gabor

I shall marry in haste and repeast at leisure.

James Branch Cabell

Wedlock: The deep, deep peace of the double bed after the hurly-burly of the chaise lounge.

Mrs Patrick Campbell

A certain sort of talent is indispensable for people who would spend years together and not bore themselves to death.

Robert Louis Stevenson

The chain of wedlock is so heavy that it takes two to carry it — sometimes three.

Alexandre Dumas

It destroys one's nerves to be amiable every day to the same human being.

Benjamin Disraeli

Marriage, n. The state or condition of a community consisting of a master, a mistress and two slaves, making in all two.
The Devil's Dictionary, Ambrose Bierce

Medieval marriages were entirely a matter of property, and, as everyone knows, marriage without love means love without marriage.
Kenneth Clark

The value of marriage is not that adults produce children but that children produce adults.
Peter de Vries

The best part of married life is the fights. The rest is merely so-so.
Thornton Wilder

No man is genuinely happy, married, who has to drink worse gin than he used to drink when he was single.
H. L. Mencken

All tragedies are finished by a death/All comedies are ended by a marriage.
Byron

Marriage has many pains, but celibacy has no pleasures.
Samuel Johnson

Wives are young men's mistresses, companions for middle age, and old men's nurses.
Francis Bacon

Courtship to marriage, is a very witty prologue to a very dull play.
William Congreve

There are four stages to a marriage. First there's the affair, then the marriage, then children and finally the fourth stage, without which you cannot know a woman, the divorce.
  Norman Mailer

Marriage is a lottery.
  English proverb

Marry in haste and repent at leisure.
  English proverb

Marriages are made in heaven.
  English proverb

The one point on which all women are in furious secret rebellion against the existing law is the saddling of the right to a child with the obligation to become the servant of a man.
  Getting Married, George Bernard Shaw

Marriage is popular because it combines the maximum of temptation with the maximum of opportunity.
  George Bernard Shaw

It is a woman's business to get married as soon as possible, and a man's to keep unmarried as long as he can.
  George Bernard Shaw

Media

The broads who work in the press are the hookers of the press. I might offer them a buck and a half.
  Frank Sinatra

Newspaper editors are men who separate the wheat from the chaff, and then print the chaff.
  Adlai Stevenson

When a dog bites a man that is not news but when a man bites a dog that is news.
John B. Bogart

This is a dull life, and the only excuse for the existence of newspapers is that they should make it less dull.
Peter Fleming

Reporters are puppets. They simply respond to the pull of the most powerful strings.
Lyndon B. Johnson

Freedom of the press in Britain is freedom to print such of the proprietor's prejudices as the advertisers don't object to.
Hannen Swaffer

The modern newspaper is half ads and the other half lies between the ads.
Anon

In the old days men had the rack. Now they have the press.
The Soul of Man Under Socialism, Oscar Wilde

Journalism is literature in a hurry.
Matthew Arnold

As for modern journalism, it is not my business to defend it. It justifies its own existence by the great Darwinian principle of survival of the vulgarest.
Intentions, Oscar Wilde

Journalism largely consists in saying "Lord Jones Dead" to people who never knew Lord Jones was alive.
G.K. Chesterton

Literature is the art of writing something that will be read twice; journalism what will be grasped at once.
Enemies of Promise, Cyril Connolly

I call journalism everything that will interest less tomorrow than it does today.
Andre Gide

Journalists say a thing that they know isn't true, in that hope that if they keep on saying it long enough it will be true.
Arnold Bennett

It is only fair to state, with regard to modern journalists, that they always apologise to one in private for what they have written against one in public.
The Soul of Man Under Socialism, Oscar Wilde

Journalism — a profession whose business it is to explain to others what it personally does not understand.
Lord Northcliffe

Politics

I captured some of the people who tried to assassinate me. I ate them before they ate me.
Idi Amin

I am proud to be called a pig. It stands for pride, integrity and guts.
Ronald Reagan

I would not like to be a Russian leader, they never know when they are being taped.
Richard Nixon

The radical of one century is the conservative of the next.
Notebooks, Mark Twain

You don't have to tell deliberate lies; but sometimes you have to be evasive.
Margaret Thatcher

Politicians are the same all over. They promise to build a bridge even when there's no river.
Nikita Khrushchev

You can't fool all of the people all of the time.
Abraham Lincoln

Since a politician never believes what he says, he is surprised when others believe him.
General Charles de Gaulle

Kissing babies gives me asthma.
John F. Kennedy

How can anyone govern a country that has 246 different kinds of cheese?
General Charles de Gaulle

I reject the cynical view that politics is inevitably, or even usually, a dirty business.
Richard Nixon

Politics makes strange bedfellows.
English proverb

I have come to the conclusion that politics are too serious a matter to be left to the politicians.
General Charles de Gaulle

A week is a long time in politics.
Sir Harold Wilson

What Englishman will give his mind to politics as long as he can afford to keep a motor car?
George Bernard Shaw

Politics is perhaps the only profession for which no profession is thought necessary.
Robert Louis Stevenson

The more cant there is in politics the better.
Aldous Huxley

There is no gambling like politics.
Benjamin Disraeli

Communism is like prohibition, it's a good idea but it won't work.
Will Rogers

For us in Russia, communism is a dead dog, while, for many people in the West it is still a living lion.
Alexander Solzhenitsyn

Every communist has a fascist frown, every fascist has a communist smile.
Muriel Spark

It's not the voting that's democracy, it's the counting.
Jumpers, *Tom Stoppard*

In an autocracy, one person has his way; in an aristocracy a few people have their way; in a democracy no one has his way.
The Decline and Fall of Science, *Celia Green*

Democracy simply means the bludgeoning of the people by the people for the people.
Oscar Wilde

Democracy substitutes election by the incompetent many for appointment by the corrupt few.
George Bernard Shaw

In those days we had a real political democracy led by a hierarchy of statesmen and not a fluid mass distracted by newspapers.
My Early Life, Winston S. Churchill

The typical socialist...a prim little man with a white-collar job, usually a secret teetotaller and often with vegetarian leanings.
The Road to Wigan Pier, George Orwell

Socialism is nothing but the capitalism of the lower classes.
Oswald Spengler

To the ordinary working man, the sort you would meet in any pub on Saturday night, Socialism does not mean much more than better wages and shorter hours and nobody bossing you about.
The Road to Wigan Pier, George Orwell

As with the Christian religion, the worst advertisement for Socialism is its adherents.
The Road to Wigan Pier, George Orwell

Socialists treat their servants with respect and then wonder why they vote Conservative. So unintelligent.
Tom Stoppard

Every country has the government it deserves.
Joseph De Maistre

Religion

I can tell you that God is alive because I talked to him this morning.
  Billy Graham

God is a gentleman. He prefers blondes.
  Joe Orton

I think God is groovy. He had a great publicity agent.
  P. J. Proby

God is love, but get it in writing.
  Gypsy Rose Lee

I am an atheist still, thank God.
  Luis Bunuel

If only God would give me a clear sign! Like making a large deposit in my name at a Swiss bank.
  Woody Allen

Not only is there no God, but try getting a plumber on the weekend.
  Woody Allen

The chief contribution of Protestantism to human thought is its massive proof that God is a bore.
  H. L. Mencken

God never wrought miracles to convince atheism, because his ordinary works convince it.
  Francis Bacon

God is for men and religion for women.
  Joseph Conrad

If Christ were here now there is one thing he would not be — a Christian.
Notebook, Mark Twain

Christianity is the most materialistic of all great religions.
Archbishop William Temple

People may say what they like about the decay of Christianity; the religious system that produced green Chartreuse can never really die.
Saki (H H. Munro)

There are many who stay away from church these days because you hardly ever mention God any more.
Arthur Miller

Don't stay away from the church because there are so many hypocrites. There's always room for one more.
A.R. Adams

Every day people are straying away from the church and going back to God. Really.
Lenny Bruce

I was just thinking, if it is really religion with these nudist colonies, they sure must turn atheists in the wintertime.
Will Rogers

Religion...is the opium of the masses.
Karl Marx

Religion is a way of walking, not a way of talking.
W.R. Inge

Religions change; beer and wine remain.
Hervey Allen

I cant talk religion to a man with bodily hunger in his eyes.
George Bernard Shaw

I am a millionaire. That is my religion.
George Bernard Shaw

Science/Technology

I don't believe in mathematics.
Albert Einstein

I do not fear computers. I fear the lack of them.
Isaac Asimov

Science is nothing but trained and organised common sense.
T. H. Huxley

Books must follow sciences, and not sciences books.
Francis Bacon

As far as the laws of mathematics refer to reality, they are not certain, and as far as they are certain, they do not refer to reality.
Albert Einstein

A science is any discipline in which the fool of this generation can go beyond the point reached by the genius of the last generation.
Max Gluckman

Science, at bottom, is really anti-intellectual. It always distrusts pure reason, and demands the production of objective fact.
H.L. Mencken

Science in the modern world has many uses; its chief use, however, is to provide long words to cover the errors of the rich. The word "kleptomania" is a vulgar example of what I mean.
  G.K. Chesterton

Traditional scientific method has always been at the very best, 20-20 hindsight. It's good for seeing where you've been.
  Robert M. Pirsig

There are no such things as applied sciences, only applications of science.
  Louis Pasteur

Sex

I've tried several varieties of sex. The conventional position makes me claustrophobic. And the others either give me a stiff neck or lockjaw.
  Tallulah Bankhead

Love is the answer, but while you are waiting for the answer, sex raises some pretty good questions.
  Woody Allen

Sex, treated properly can be one of the most gorgeous things in the world.
  Elizabeth Taylor

Whoever called it necking was a poor judge of anatomy.
  Groucho Marx

Only good girls keep diaries, bad girls don't have the time.
  Tallulah Bankhead

Chastity — the most unnatural of the sexual perversions.
  Aldous Huxley

Continental people have sex life; the English have hot water bottles.
  George Mikes

Sex is only the liquid centre of the great Newberry Fruit of friendship.
  Super-Jilly, Jilly Cooper

All this fuss about sleeping together. For physical pleasure I'd sooner go to my dentist any day.
  Vile Bodies, Evelyn Waugh

Familiarity breeds contempt — and children.
  Notebooks, Mark Twain

I am not promiscuous, you know. Promiscuity implies that attraction is not necessary.
  Tallulah Bankhead

Pornography is the attempt to insult sex, to do dirt on it.
  D. H. Lawrence

If God had meant us to have group sex, I guess he'd have given us all more organs.
  Who Do You Think You Are, "A Very Hospitable Person", Malcolm Bradbury

Sometimes I think that if there was a third sex men wouldn't get so much as a glance from me.
  Love Me Little, Amanda Vail

Is sex dirty? Only if it's done right.
  From film, All You've Ever Wanted to Know About Sex, Woody Allen

I regard sex like a glass of water, from which I drink when I'm thirsty *(Alexandra Kollontai to Lenin)*
But who wants to drink a glass of dirty water? *(Lenin)*

Don't knock it, it's sex with someone you love.
Woody Allen on masturbation

Masturbation: the primary sexual activity of mankind. In the nineteenth century it was a disease; in the twentieth, it's a cure.
Thomas Szasz

The nearest I've been to a sexual experience lately is finding lipstick on a cafe cup.
The Secret Lemonade Drinker, Guy Bellamy

It was the most fun I ever had without laughing.
Annie Hall, Woody Allen on sex

Sex is one of the nine reasons for re-incarnation...The other eight are unimportant.
Big Sur and the Oranges of Hieronymous Bosch, Henry Miller

Travel

Too often travel, instead of broadening the mind, merely lengthens the conversation.
Elizabeth Drew

I dislike feeling at home when I am abroad.
George Bernard Shaw

Holidays are often overrated disturbances of routine, costly and uncomfortable, and they usually need another holiday to correct their ravages.
E. V. Lucas

But why, oh why, do the wrong people travel when the right people stay at home?
Sail Away, Noel Coward.

Writing about travels is nearly always tedious, travelling being, like war and fornication, exciting but not interesting.
Malcolm Muggeridge

For my part, I travel not to go anywhere, but to go. I travel for travel's sake. The great affair is to move.
Travels with a Donkey, Robert Louis Stevenson

Travel broadens the mind.
English proverb

Travel makes a wise man better, but a fool worse.
English proverb

War

The first casualty when war comes is truth.
Hiram Johnson, American Senator

They shall not pass.
General Petain, Verdun

Jaw-jaw is better than war-war.
Harold Macmillan

Talking jaw to jaw is better than going to war.
Winston S. Churchill

Frankly, I'd like to see the government get out of war altogether and leave the whole field to private industry.
Joseph Heller

The quickest way of ending a war is to lose it.
Shooting an Elephant, George Orwell

War is like love, it always finds a way.
Bertolt Brecht

My argument is that War makes rattling good history; but Peace is poor reading.
Thomas Hardy

War is delightful to those who have had not experience of it.
Erasmus

No country without any atom bomb could properly consider itself independent.
Charles de Gaulle

We are going to have peace even if we have to fight for it.
Dwight D. Eisenhower

I love war and responsibility and excitement. Peace is going to be hell on me.
General George S. Patton

Either war is obsolete, or men are.
R. Buckminster Fuller

There never was a good war, or a bad peace.
Benjamin Franklin

You can't say civilisation don't advance, however, for in every war they kill you in a new way.
Will Rogers

If we lose this war, I'll start another in my wife's name.
Moshe Dayan

War is capitalism with the gloves off.
Tom Stoppard

All may begin a war, few can end it.
English proverb

If you want peace, you must prepare for war.
English proverb

As long as war is regarded as wicked, it will always have its fascination. When it is looked upon as vulgar, it will cease to be popular.
Oscar Wilde